AF583013

DECIDE WISELY

Illustrated Sayings to Guide Your Path

ARTURO JOSE SANCHEZ HERNANDEZ

2024

DECIDE WISELY

First edition. September 5, 2024.

Written by Arturo José Sánchez Hernández.

DEDICATION

To all those who seek clarity and wisdom on their path. May these illustrated sayings serve as a beacon in times of doubt and a source of inspiration in moments of hope. I dedicate this book to those who choose each day to grow, learn, and move forward with an open heart and a curious mind.

Contents

PROLOGUE TO THE FIRST EDITION IN SPANISH

Our decisions, whether good or bad, define the course of our lives. Sometimes, we blame luck or fate for what is, unfortunately, nothing more than the result of poor decisions made at significant moments in our personal existence. There are times when a single moment of confusion can forever change our individual future, leading us to failure, "burning the ships," and dragging us into a journey with no return. "Ah... if only I had done what I should have... I shouldn't have acted without thinking, without considering other options... I was foolish... why am I so indecisive?"

Take a moment, dear reader, to reflect on how much suffering or happiness past decisions have brought into your life; you will then realize the importance of incorporating grains of wisdom about making the right choices, which are compiled in this book.

For psychiatrists, psychologists, educators, general practitioners... for anyone who wants to be a good psychotherapist, this is an essential work. But it's not written solely for communication professionals; it's an effective tool for anyone's personal development. It's useful, pleasant to read, and accessible to everyone.

I have had the privilege of writing the prologue and recommending several books by Dr. Arturo Sánchez in recent years. I am pleased to do so because he is the most brilliant and prolific representative of the new generation of therapists trained in the Camagüey school of psychotherapy, which is fundamentally based on the role of attitude and the formation of values and moral qualities for therapeutic change and personal development. This book is an important contribution by the author in this direction. He does it with talent, modesty, and originality. I quickly recognized him as a scientific promise for the specialty as soon as I took on the honorable task of introducing him, accompanying him, and mentoring him in his studies and research on concrete attitude psychotherapy. The future will have many positive things to say about his role in Cuban psychiatry and psychotherapy.

Read "Decide Wisely" carefully. You will enjoy it and appreciate the time invested.

DrC. Alberto Clavijo Portieles.

Honorary Member of the Cuban Society of Psychiatry.

~~~

PREFACE TO THE SECOND EDITION IN SPANISH

In *"Decide Wisely: Illustrated Sayings to Guide Your Path,"* we invite you on a unique journey where ancient popular wisdom and visual power come together to illuminate the art of decision-making. This book is a practical and enriching guide that uses sayings from various cultures and eras, accompanied by evocative illustrations, to provide you with tools and perspectives that will help you make decisions with greater clarity and confidence.

Each chapter is dedicated to a key aspect of decision-making, from intuition and logic to patience and action. Sayings, known for their ability to encapsulate great truths in few words, are broken down and explained in their original context to show their relevance in today's world. The images, created with artificial intelligence and carefully selected, enrich the messages conveyed by the sayings, offering a visual experience that facilitates deeper reflection and understanding.

This book is not only a practical tool for improving decision-making skills but also a source of daily inspiration and wisdom.

Decide Wisely is ideal for anyone looking to make more accurate and meaningful decisions, whether in the personal, professional, or emotional sphere. Let the wisdom of the sayings and the beauty of the illustrations guide your path towards wiser and more conscious decisions.

The Author.

~~~

PREFACE TO THE FIRST EDITION IN ENGLISH

In this third edition of *"Decide Wisely: Illustrated Sayings to Guide Your Path"*, we have enriched the original Spanish content to make it accessible to a global audience, combining the timeless wisdom of sayings with evocative illustrations that deepen the understanding of the art of decision-making.

In the first edition, the text served as a valuable guide for making decisions, but the simple images did not fully capture the depth of the book's message.

In the second edition, we incorporated AI-generated illustrations that brought the sayings to life, enhancing the reader's experience and fostering a deeper understanding of the messages.

Now, in this third edition, we have carefully translated and adapted the content into English, maintaining the original essence while expanding its reach to a global audience. The sayings, as the cornerstone of this work, remain as powerful as ever, and the illustrations continue to guide the reader's reflection and understanding.

Whether you are encountering this work for the first time or revisiting it with fresh eyes, *Decide Wisely* is designed to be a companion on your journey toward more informed and accurate decisions. May the wisdom of the sayings and the beauty of the illustrations guide you as you navigate the complexities of life with clarity and confidence.

Dr. Arturo José Sánchez Hernández.

Author.

~~~

INTRODUCTION

Nothing influences a person's life more repeatedly, and with greater impact on their quality of life, than the act of making decisions. The achievement of happiness and fulfillment largely depends on this process, while the source of great suffering often lies in poor decisions that could have been avoided or in failing to make certain decisions that were urgently needed.

There is an entire theory dedicated to decision-making, to which many branches of science have contributed, including neurophysiology, psychology, sociology, political science, game theory, and systems theory, among many others. This theory has applications in multiple fields, such as the military, economics, politics, medicine, education, and even in managing one's own life.

In every profession or trade, a set of knowledge and skills is taught to guide individuals in making the best decisions in that specific area. Each ethical theory prescribes how decisions should be made. This presents a challenge when trying to establish historical precedents: decision theory cannot be as extensive as the history of human knowledge itself. Nevertheless, significant contributions within the analyzed theory can be mentioned.

In ancient times, the Athenian military historian Thucydides (460 B.C. - 396-? B.C.), in *The History of the Peloponnesian War,*[1] examines the factors that led leaders to make state decisions, addressing both the characteristics of the environment and the interests that motivated them.

In the modern era, the Italian diplomat, politician, and writer Niccolò Machiavelli (1469–1527), in *The Prince,*[2] a work considered pioneering in the field of political science, explains the decisions that rulers have made throughout history to maintain power and uphold the interests of the state.

During this same historical period, the French mathematician, physicist, philosopher, and theologian Blaise Pascal (1623-1662), in his work *Pensées*3, addresses decision-making in situations of uncertainty.

In contemporary times, there has been an abundance of works on the subject. For example, the American economist, political scientist, and sociologist Herbert Alexander Simon (1916–2001), in *Models of Man: Social and Rational; Mathematical Essays on Rational Human Behavior in a Society Setting*4, points out that the rationality of most people is limited due to cognitive constraints of the individual mind, as well as insufficiencies in the information and time available to make decisions.

Nothing influences a person's life more repeatedly, and has a greater impact on their quality of life, than making decisions. The achievement of happiness and fulfillment largely depends on this process, while the origin of great suffering often lies in poor decisions that could have been avoided, or in the failure to make decisions that needed to be made.

There is an entire theory dedicated to decision-making, contributed to by many branches of science, including neurophysiology, psychology, sociology, political science, game theory, and systems theory, among others. This theory has applications in various fields such as the military, economics, politics, medicine, education, and even in managing one's own existence.

In every profession or trade, a set of knowledge and skills is taught to help make the best decisions in that area, and each ethical theory prescribes how decisions should be made. This raises a problem when trying to establish historical precedents: decision theory cannot be as extensive as the entire history of human knowledge. However, we can still mention significant contributions within the analyzed theory.

In antiquity, the Athenian military historian Thucydides (460 BC - 396? BC), in *"The History of the Peloponnesian War,"* examines the factors that led leaders to make state decisions, addressing both the characteristics of the environment and the interests that motivated them.

In the modern era, the Italian diplomat, politician, and writer Niccolò Machiavelli (1469-1527), in *"The Prince,"* a work considered pioneering in the field of political science, explains the decisions that rulers have made throughout history to stay in power and protect the state's interests.

During this same historical period, the French mathematician, physicist, philosopher, and theologian Blaise Pascal (1623-1662) in his work *"Pensées"* addresses decision-making in situations of uncertainty.

In contemporary times, there has been a wealth of work on the subject. For example, the American economist, political scientist, and sociologist Herbert Alexander Simon (1916–2001), in *"Models of Man: Social and Rational; Mathematical Essays on Rational Human Behavior in Society Setting,"*[4] points out that most people's rationality is limited due to the cognitive constraints of the individual mind, as well as insufficiencies in the information and time available to make decisions.

The American mathematician John Forbes Nash (1928-2015), a Nobel laureate in Economics in 1994, in *Non-Cooperative Games,*[5] proposed what has been called the "Nash Equilibrium," which shows how collaborative decisions can be much more effective for everyone than those made solely to maximize individual benefits.

The American psychologist Barry Schwartz (1946-), in *The Paradox of Choice: Why More is Less,*[6] argues that autonomy and freedom of choice are fundamental to well-being. However, having more options, rather than providing freedom, can lead to paralysis; and the more alternatives one has to choose from, the less satisfied one is with the decisions made. Therefore, reducing options can lessen buyers' anxiety. Schwartz also proposes the following steps as necessary for consumers to make good decisions: Calculate the goals or objectives, assess the importance of each goal, rank the options, evaluate the likelihood that each option will meet the objectives, choose the winning option, and modify the goals.

The economist and Nobel laureate in Economics Richard H. Thaler (1945-) and the lawyer Cass R. Sunstein (1954-), both Americans, joined forces in *Nudge: Improving Decisions About Health, Wealth, and Happiness,*[7] where they critique the idea that humans reason and choose perfectly. They describe two systems that characterize human thinking: the automatic system, which is fast and instinctive, and the reflective system, which is deliberate and conscious. The book explains various types of biases and offers important elements that help improve personal decisions related to health, well-being, and happiness.

The American economists and brothers Dan Heath (1973-) and Chip Heath (1963-), in *Decisive: How to Make Better Choices in Life and Work,*[8] discuss common mistakes made when making decisions and provide a method for improving them called WRAP, an acronym for: Widen Your Options, Reality-Test Your Assumptions, Attain Distance Before Deciding, and Prepare to Be Wrong.

The Israeli-American psychologist Daniel Kahneman (1934-), a Nobel laureate in Economics in 2002, in *Thinking, Fast and Slow,*[9] integrates aspects of psychological research into economics, particularly concerning human judgment and decision-making under uncertainty. He explains the differences between a fast, instinctive, and emotional mode of thinking and a slow, deliberative, and logical one.

The same author, along with Olivier Sibony and lawyer Cass R. Sunstein (1954-), co-authored *Noise: A Flaw in Human Judgment,*[10] a work that draws attention to the way decisions are made. They argue that around human judgments on the same issue, there is undesirable noise or variability caused by factors such as cognitive biases, moods, group dynamics, and emotional reactions, with the first being considered the most important.

The Colombian journalist, writer, and former Catholic priest Alberto Linero Gómez (1968-), in *The Power of Decisions,*[11] suggests making decisions driven by the strength of the heart, guided by reason, and based on values. He explains that it is important to consider how decisions affect others as well as oneself, and then be capable of assuming the consequences.

The Chilean economist Tirso José Alecoy, in *Decision-Making Linked to Logical Reasoning and Personality,*[12] addresses the types of decisions individuals make throughout their lives and presents useful elements to ensure they are effective and productive.

In Cuba, the physician and specialist in Internal Medicine, Luis Alberto Corona Martínez, published a series of articles under the title: *The General Theory on Decision-Making and Its Application to the Field of Medical Care I, II, and III.* In the first part,[13] he analyzes the rational and behavioral theories of decision-making. In the second part,[14] he addresses the methods and techniques for evaluating and selecting options, proposing research, cost-benefit analysis, as well as decision trees, all of which help in choosing options under the uncertainty that often characterizes this process in the medical field. In the third part,[15] he emphasizes the ethical dimension of medical decisions, describes the relationship between the types of problems and the necessary decisions in each case, and highlights the importance of experience, judgment, and creativity for making effective decisions.

Another Cuban author to consider is the psychologist and sociologist Ovidio D'Angelo Hernández, who in *Life Project and Integral Human Development*[16] offers important insights into decisions that set the course of an individual's life.

In the present study, decision-making is approached from the perspective of the moral qualities necessary to carry it out effectively; from this, the fundamental starting concepts are derived. Decision-making is understood as a process by which a decision-maker chooses between two or more possible alternatives, establishes a course of action, carries it out, verifies the results, and establishes corrective measures if necessary. Meanwhile, positive moral qualities are characteristics of an individual's personality expressed in habitual decision-making patterns that allow them to satisfactorily fulfill their functions within society and adequately guide their own personal development. However, despite this close interrelationship, the author of the present study has not found texts that link these concepts from the perspective of Cuban cultural identity.

In response to this identified gap, the main objective was set to address this relationship, for which answers to the following questions are proposed: How is the decision-making process carried out, and how can decisions be classified? What stages make up the decision-making process? What deviations can appear in each of them? What moral qualities are necessary for making sound decisions?

The work consists of an introduction, three chapters, general recommendations for making good decisions, and a system of glossaries with the most important terms used.

In the first chapter, the decision-making process is explained, and possible classifications of it are presented. The second chapter exposes the most important moral vices that can arise at each stage of this process. In contrast, the third chapter presents the moral qualities necessary for making satisfactory decisions.

The general suggestions for making good decisions provide a summary of the main ideas developed in the study. These are presented starting with a guideline or exhortation, explained concisely, and concluded with a maxim, proverb, or saying.

The glossary system is composed of compilations of terms on decision theory, decision-making psychology, game theory, ethical-moral values, and essential moral qualities present in this process.

For the preparation of this work, systematizations on decision theory and game theory were studied from authors such as the American mathematician John Forbes Nash; the American economists Richard H. Thaler and Herbert Alexander Simon, the latter also a political scientist and sociologist; the Israeli-American psychologist Daniel Kahneman; and the Colombian journalist, writer, and former Catholic priest Alberto Linero Gómez, all mentioned in the historical background of the treatment of the decision-making topic.

Classical authors in ethics were also consulted, such as Aristotle,[17] Plato,[18] Seneca,[19] and Socrates,[20] as well as recent researchers in the field of value theory, like the Argentine philosopher and anthropologist Risieri Frondizi,[21] and from Cuba: the philosopher José Ramón Fabelo Corzo,[22] the educator Esther Báxter Pérez,[23] and the psychologist Fernando González Rey.[24]

Regarding the maxims and proverbs, texts such as the Bible,[25] the Tao Teh Ching by Lao Tzu,[26] the Analects of Confucius,[27] the Panchatantra by Vishnu Sarma,[28] Maxims, Exhortations, and Advice by Epictetus,[29] as well as the works of José Martí30 were reviewed.

Sayings from different regions of the world were collected. For instance, those of Spanish origin were extracted from *Refranes, Proverbios, Dichos y Sentencias: Todo el Tesoro de la Sabiduría Popular de los Pueblos de España a su Alcance*[31] by José Antonio Solís, and *Diccionario de Aforismos, Proverbios y Refranes*[32] by Jorge Sintes Pros; Chilean sayings from *Refranes Chilenos*[33] by Agustín Cannobbio; Mexican sayings from *Dichos o Refranes: Compendio Temático*[34] by Samuel Flores-Huerta; and Cuban sayings from *El Libro de los Refranes*[35] by Tomás Álvarez de los Ríos, *Del Piropo al Dicharacho: Folklore Oral de Cuba*[36], *El Saber y el Cantar de Juan sin Nada*[37], and *El Saber de Juan sin Nada*[38], all by Cuban researcher Samuel Feijóo, with the third also including sayings from different countries.

Afro-Cuban sayings were mainly compiled from *Refranes Adivinatorios del Caracol y de los Odun de Ifá en la Santería Cubana*[39] by Ernesto Valdés Jane, along with others heard by the author from the daily conversations of Cuban men and women.

The images, on the other hand, were created with the assistance of the artificial intelligence DALL-E3.

As a novel feature of the product, the work offers a link between decision theory and ethical-moral values theory, as well as the unique structure of the work itself. Based on theoretical arguments about the moral qualities necessary at each stage of the decision-making process, the work integrates resources such as sayings, proverbs, images, and glossaries of terms, which complement one another, thus enhancing the understanding of the topic addressed.

The work deals with moral qualities of extraordinary relevance for proper social performance, making it a potentially useful reference material for those who cultivate these qualities in their professional work.

It could contribute to the development of courses with an ethical-axiological and psychiatric profile, elevate the general culture of the population through the dissemination of its findings, and meet the growing and urgent demand for literature on the theory of ethical-moral values.

The compilation of guiding and inspiring reflections also makes the work suitable as self-help material for readers, and as an auxiliary text for those practicing psychotherapy.

Answers are proposed to many questions that may arise at any age but are frequent and intense during adolescence. Therefore, this work could also be useful as a supplementary text for those who work with individuals in this age group.

After presenting the reader with brief historical background on the topic, the positions and sources adopted for the creation of the work, as well as its innovations, intended audience, and potential beneficiaries, it is now fully offered for your consideration.

~~~

Chapter I. DECISION-MAKING PROCESS

This chapter presents possible classifications of the decision-making process and explains the stages that make it up.

CLASSIFICATION OF DECISIONS

Decisions can be classified in multiple ways, and we will present a few that are relevant for better understanding.

Importance

Momentous Decisions: Their execution has substantial consequences on significant aspects of the decision-maker's life. These are not frequent.

Trivial Decisions: Their consequences do not affect important aspects of the decision-maker's life or do so in an insignificant way.

Between these two extremes lies a range of decisions with varying levels of importance. This requires setting an order of priorities, as not all decisions can be made at the same time.

– *"You can't blow and sip at the same time."*

– *"Want to improve your life? Improve your priorities."*

– *"Give importance to what's important."*

– *"Priority to what truly matters."*

Giving and Giving, the Drip Wears Away (Spain)[40]

Momentous decisions, due to their great impact on one's life, clearly require full attention. While trivial decisions may seem like they can be ignored, reality shows otherwise. Decisions that today produce insignificant results, when repeated over time, have a cumulative effect that can lead to significant consequences.

–*"Many littles make a lot." (Spain)*[41]

–*"Add a grain each day, and soon you'll have a heap." (Spain)*[42]

–*"Small things grow big if they persist." (Afro-Cuban Saying)*[43]

–*"Grain by grain, the granary fills up." (Spain)*[44]

–*"One grain doesn't make a granary, but it helps its neighbor." (Spain)*[45]

–*"Drop by drop, the sea is drained." (Galicia, Spain)*[46]

–*"Soft water on hard stone, with persistence, makes a hole." (Spain)*[47]

These progressively accumulating results can be for the good. Many great goals are not achieved all at once, but little by little.

–*"Step by step, one goes far." (Spain)*[48]

–*"Little by little, the old woman climbs the coconut tree." (San Salvador)*[49]

–*"Hammering away, the blacksmith refines his work." (Spain)*[50]

–*Similarly, many deviations don't happen in a single day but over time.*

–*"Deviations that start off by centimeters can eventually stretch into kilometers."*

–*"He who neglects small things will end up in ruin." (Ecclesiasticus: 19,1)*[51]

–*"Whoever despises the little, will later suffer the great." (Chile)*[52]

This is why attention must be paid not only to decisions and habits that bring about immediate, significant consequences, but which are generally infrequent, as well as those with seemingly insignificant effects but that are carried out daily.

–*"Watch your habits."*

–*"Break the leg of a bad habit." (Spain)*[53]

–*"A hobby that harms more than it helps should be quickly discarded." (Spain)*[54]

–*"What's unnecessary is too much; leave it behind." (Spain)*[55]

–*"What's useless, toss it out." (Cuba)*[56]

–*"To strengthen a tree, you must prune it." (Tibet)*[57]

Immediacy

Urgent or Non-Postponable: These need immediate attention as failing to do so may lead to very undesirable consequences.

Non-Urgent or Postponable: These can wait to be executed.

Some decisions that impact important aspects of life don't need to be made urgently, while neglecting those that require immediate attention may lead to negative consequences, so they will always have some degree of importance.

–*"What's urgent isn't always the most important, and what's most important isn't always urgent."*

However, the level of importance of urgent matters is sometimes low, and being overwhelmed by these could lead to dangerously postponing momentous decisions that, while important, can be delayed.

–*"Don't lose sight of the postponable, momentous things for the sake of unimportant urgent matters."*

Another point to consider is that decisions requiring immediacy can lead to hasty actions.

–*"Too much haste exposes us to error."*

–*"He who rushes delays or loses."*

In addition, traps may hide behind these decisions, relying precisely on the limited time a hurried person has to weigh the possible negative consequences.

–*"A rushed man doesn't see the trap."*

–*"A rushed man lacks wisdom." (Cuba)*[58]

There is a time to go slow and a time to go fast.

Each decision, in turn, has its own demands regarding the time in which it must be made and executed. While some must be made quickly, others require a prudent wait.

–*"Going fast has its advantages, going slow has its advantages." (African Proverb)*[59]

–*"Everything in its time."*

–*"In this world, everything has its hour; there is a time for everything that happens." (Ecclesiastes: 3,1)*[60]

–*"Each thing in its own time." (Spain)*[61]

Rationality

Rational Decisions: Deliberation over options is carried out thoughtfully and objectively before deciding.

Emotional Decisions: Reflection on the alternatives has been somewhat distorted by emotions.

Impulsive Decisions: These are made without reflection or caution, driven by impulses and the impression of the moment.

Affectivity is a significant part of human existence, to the point that if an individual doesn't feel emotionally invested in a piece of knowledge or doesn't feel it as a conviction, it will serve little purpose. It's unlikely they will put it into practice, and if they do, it will be reluctantly.

–*"Knowledge without heart leads nowhere."*

Love and Knowledge, Together They Cannot Be (Spain)[62]

While the emotional drive is essential for decision-making, it can also distort, to some extent, our subjective view of reality and reasoning, making it difficult to make impartial judgments.

–*"The more one loves, fears, or hates, the less they judge."*

–*"Love, hate, and fear exaggerate." (Hebrew Saying)*[63]

–*"The heart rules the eyes, making them 'trick-eyes.'" (Spain)*[64]

–*"Love, like fear, makes one believe everything."*

On the other hand, the capacity and time available to seek the necessary information for decision-making are always limited, which affects the quality of those decisions.

–*"Quick decisions are usually insecure."*

Considering these peculiarities of human nature and the circumstances in which decisions must be made, some decisions are based on an objective reflection of the available information.

- *"When passions such as joy, anger, and pleasure have not awakened, that is our central or moral self." (Confucius)*[65]
- *"Achieving central harmony is certainly the most significant human accomplishment. For a long time, people have been unable to reach it." (Confucius)*[66]

In others, reasoning is greatly influenced by emotions, leading to poor judgment.

- *"When passions blind, reasoning becomes unnecessary." (Spain)*[67]
- *"When we are disturbed by anger, the heart is not in its rightful place; when blinded by love, the heart is not in its rightful place; when enveloped by worries and anxieties, the heart is not in its rightful place, and the spirit has lost its balance." (Confucius)*[68]

Acting Without Thinking is Like Shooting Without Aiming

In some cases, there's not even any reflection.

–*"Acting without thinking can make us stumble."*

–*"Don't go for the first option." (Afro-Cuban Saying)*[69]

Complexity

Simple Decisions: These involve few elements or variables to consider, making their potential consequences few and easy to predict.

Complex Decisions: These involve many elements or variables, making their consequences unpredictable or very difficult to foresee.

Simple decisions can be found in controlled, experimental conditions, as generally, most decisions involve many interacting elements in various ways, whose complexity makes prediction difficult.

–*"From under any old palm leaf comes a big scorpion." (Santo Domingo)*[70]

–*"Out of any nougat, a mouse comes jumping." (Cuba)*[71]

Reversibility

Reversible Decisions: After being implemented, one can return to the situation as it was before.

Partially Reversible Decisions: Only some elements of their consequences can be restored.

Irreversible Decisions: Once made, you cannot go back to the previous situation.

He Who Went to Seville Lost His Chair (Spain)[72]

Since everything is in constant change and evolution, the circumstances to which one can return after a decision will never be exactly the same in every aspect. After some decisions, it may be possible to return to a situation with similar options, while with others, the chosen path may completely block any possibility of going back.

–*"He who strays too far loses the way back." (Afro-Cuban Saying)73*

Number of People Involved

Individual Decisions: These are made by one person without the collaboration or influence of others.

Group Decisions: These are made by two or more people.

Free the Ideas, But Seal the Lips (Egypt)[74]

Individual decisions have the advantage of being made in secret, which helps avoid alerting potential competition.

– *"He who does it alone, pays for it alone."*

– *"If you don't want noise, don't drag dry leaves." (Cuba)*[75]

However, their downside is that they rely solely on the knowledge and experience of the individual, without the benefit of other perspectives to complement the decision.

– *"One hand alone cannot clap."*

– *"A single finger cannot catch a louse." (African Saying)*[76]

– *"With one arm, you cannot carry two watermelons."*

– *"With one hand, you cannot tie a knot." (Panchatantra)*[77]

– *"One stick alone doesn't make a forest." (Afro-Cuban Saying)*[78]

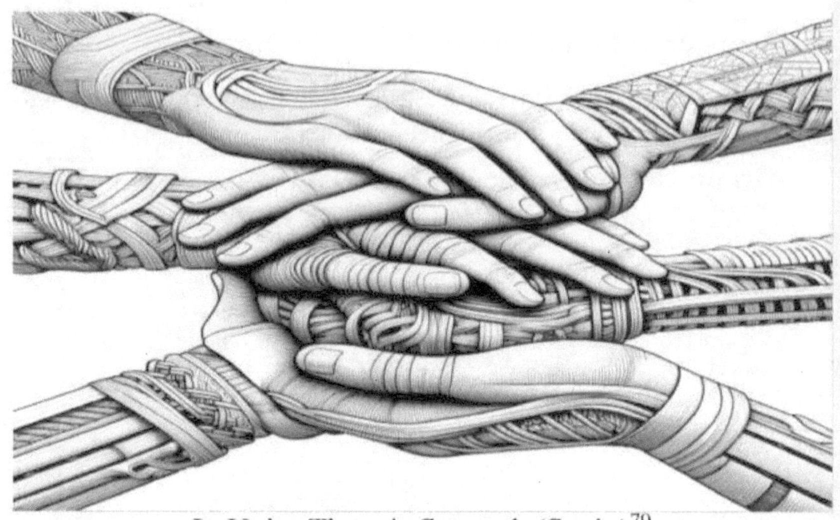

In Unity There is Strength (Spain)[79]

Group decisions allow for the benefit of combining the specific knowledge and experience of each group member, resulting in a more well-rounded and integrated decision.

–*"Two heads are better than one." (Mexico)*[80]

–*"The coals heat each other." (Czechoslovakia)*[81]

–*"Many hands make light work."*

When the Fox Preaches, Watch Your Chickens (Germany)[82]

The downside of **group decisions** is that each participant has their own interests, which will influence their reasoning and arguments.

- *"Self-interest rules the world." (Spain)*[83]
- *"Everyone wants to bring water to their own mill and leave their neighbor's dry." (Spain)*[84]
- *"It's easy to preach fasting after you've just eaten." (Spain)*[85]
- *"When the fox preaches, the chickens aren't safe." (Spain)*[86]

A Secret Between Two is No Secret (Afro-Cuban Saying)[87]

Making projects public can lead to losing the element of surprise.

–*"A secret between three is no secret." (Spain)*[88]

–*"A shared secret is a lost secret." (Afro-Cuban Saying)*[89]

Frequency with Which Decisions Must Be Made

Routine Decisions: These are made to solve repetitive or recurring problems that are relatively well-known, turning them into routine actions.

Sporadic Decisions: These are made to solve less frequent problems, where there is little experience.

Novel Decisions: These are made to address new problems for which no prior experience exists.

Just because problems are sporadic doesn't mean there aren't established rules or procedures to solve them; however, their infrequency usually means there is little to no experience in handling them.

Levels of Generalization of the Goals They Aim to Achieve

Strategic Decisions: These set the most general objectives that guide the life of an individual or group.

Tactical Decisions: These define the intermediate objectives to achieve the strategic ones.

Operational Decisions: These specify the concrete activities needed to fulfill the tactical decisions, to which they are subordinate.

Among tactical or intermediate goals, there may be varying levels of generalization, where some could be considered a means to reach more general goals, which, in turn, are means to reach even more general ones, leading up to the strategic ones. This hierarchy flows from the strategic to the operational.

The more general a goal is, the more it provides a sense of direction, but it offers fewer details about how to achieve it, which is where less general goals come in. Understanding the most general or strategic objectives helps clarify the importance of achieving the tactical ones, improving improvisation skills and preventing confusion or failure in prioritizing and sequencing.

– *"When the general principles are determined beforehand, there will be no confusion when it's time to act." (Confucius)*[90]

Knowing the operational objectives makes behavior more effective in reaching the tactical and strategic goals.

– *"Ends without means are empty, and means without an end are blind."*

Existence of Established Procedures for Problem-Solving

Programmed Decisions: There are socially established rules or procedures for addressing the problems, so they don't need to be re-examined every time a decision is made.

Semi-Programmed Decisions: Existing norms or rules help solve part of the problem but don't completely resolve it, requiring the creation of additional solutions.

Non-Programmed Decisions: These address problems for which there are no clear rules or procedures, so new ones must be developed entirely.

In every culture or social organization, there are rules or norms to solve specific problems, whether an individual knows them or not. Others, being new to that society, will lack these references for their solution.

Even though there aren't specific procedures to solve non-programmed problems, there are still general rules for making decisions of any kind. Semi-programmed and non-programmed decisions require innovation, and there is a risk of trying to inappropriately apply rules that work well for programmed ones.

Existence of Knowledge and Skills for Problem-Solving

Structured Decisions: The necessary knowledge and skills to solve the problems are fully available.

Semi-Structured Decisions: There is a partial level of knowledge and skills, which need to be supplemented until they become fully operational.

Unstructured Decisions: These lack the required knowledge and skills, so they must be sought out or developed.

In general, for routine or repetitive problems, there are high levels of information and skills to face them, or at least, that is the ideal to strive for.

– *"Master the routine aspects of your business."*

– *"No good bird gets shot twice on the same branch."*

The Goad Pulls the Ox from the Mud (Cuba)[91]

However, new problems often arise for which the available resources, whether psychological or otherwise, are insufficient to resolve. These problems can cause high levels of discomfort, forcing the necessary changes to be made.

– *"Hot iron bends easily; the same happens with people." (Spain)*[92]

– *"When the iron is hot, that's when it must be struck." (Spain)*[93]

If You're Well, You Won't Move (Spain)[94]

These transformations wouldn't occur from a place of comfort and well-being.

– *"The blacksmith who works with cold iron, wastes time." (Spain)*[95]

Therefore, these events are not only inevitable but also necessary for personal growth.

– *"Blows teach." (Afro-Cuban Saying)*[96]

– *"No one has grown without having suffered."*

– *"He who doesn't fall, doesn't rise." (Spain)*[97]

– *"He who hasn't been tested knows little." (Ecclesiasticus: 34,10)*[98]

Some Storms Come to Clear Your Path

When faced with these types of problems, an individual can learn enough and make the necessary changes to solve them, gaining maturity and personal growth in the process.

- *"Blessed be the storm that made you grow."*
- *"Can't change a situation? Better yourself and change yourself."*
- *"Be thankful for the drop that overflowed the cup because it's the seed of the change you needed."*
- *"What once felt like a hurricane, we now see as the wind clearing the way for us."*

If You Don't Change, Everything Repeats

Or the lessons learned are insufficient or incorrect, preventing necessary changes from being made, leaving problems unsolved.

–*"Insanity is doing the same thing over and over and expecting different results."*

–*"You have two options: evolve or repeat."*

As a result, discomfort levels remain or increase, and health becomes compromised.

–*"Nothing is as painful as being stuck in the same place."*

–*"Life is change, growth is optional, choose wisely."*

–*"Change is constant, growth is optional. The choice is yours."*

Level of Emotional Commitment to Problem-Solving

High Emotional Commitment: There is a strong emotional investment in solving certain problems, experienced as a conviction.

Lack of Emotional Commitment: The need to solve problems is recognized cognitively but without any real conviction to act.

Simply knowing about the need to solve a problem doesn't guarantee action, even when all the resources are available. Without emotional engagement, one's behavior remains unchanged. If it were otherwise, therapy for an alcoholic or smoker could be reduced to simple educational talks or recommended readings.

–*"Knowledge without heart is of little use."*

Temporal Relationship with the Problems Being Solved

Proactive or Anticipatory: These decisions are made to prevent certain problems from arising or to be better prepared to face them.

Reactive: These decisions are made in response to existing problems.

Delayed or Postponed: These decisions are made too late, losing their effectiveness in solving the problems they aim to address.

When You Have the Antelope in Front of You, It's
Not the Time to Prepare the Spear (Guinea)[99]

There are foreseeable problems for which proactive measures can be taken so that when they arise, you are already prepared to face them.

–*"The strong foresee; second-rate men wait for the storm with arms crossed." (José Martí)*[100]

–*"Dig the well before you are thirsty." (China)*[101]

–*"Don't wait for the light to go out to look for matches." (Cuba)*[102]

–*"When you are thirsty, it's too late to dig a well." (Japan)*[103]

–*"Don't wait for the day of battle to sharpen your weapon." (Afro-Cuban Saying)*[104]

Better Safe Than Sorry (Czechoslovakia)[105]

Or, with the right measures in place, the problems may never arise.

- *"Some put the palm leaf down before the leak starts." (Cuba)*[106]
- *"It's better to have a 'just in case' than a 'who could have known?'" (Cuba)*[107]
- *"Patch it up before the blister forms." (Cuba)*[108]

When You're About to Fall, You Don't See the Hole (Venezuela)[109]

No one has the ability to foresee every situation that may arise, so the capacity for anticipation is always limited.

–*"There are hidden traps." (Afro-Cuban Saying)*[110]

–*"From under any palm leaf, a scorpion emerges." (Cuba)*[111]

–*"A bird takes flight right in front of your feet." (Japan)*[112]

–*"No bird knows it's going to get caught in a trap." (Afro-Cuban Saying)*[113]

–*"Anyone can get tangled in the string." (Cuba)*[114]

–*"As fish are caught in a net and birds in a trap, so are humans ensnared by misfortune when they least expect it." (Ecclesiastes 9:12)*[115]

Everything in Its Own Time (Czech Republic)[116]

We do have the responsibility to take the necessary steps when facing problems that haven't yet occurred but are foreseeable, or those that have happened and couldn't have been predicted.

– *"The remedy, in its time."*

– *"I decide according to the circumstances of the time, and I act accordingly." (Confucius)*[117]

– *"Put on the cloak as the wind blows." (Spain)*[118]

Failing to act in time results in ineffective actions when they are eventually taken.

– *"The hat arrived so late it found no head."*

– *"If the head doesn't seek a hat, when it finds one, there will be a hat, but no head." (Afro-Cuban Saying)*[119]

– *"Locking the chest after the robbery is a fool's precaution." (Spain)*[120]

– *"The parrot is dead, what do I need the cage for?" (Mexico)*[121]

– *"They ask the dead: 'Do you want it?'" (Spain)*[122]

–"Advice given too late is the same as no advice." (San Salvador)[123]

–"Now that the rabbit's gone, you give me advice?" (Spain)[124]

Sequentiality

Sequential Decisions: These follow a logical order of steps or stages for their implementation, as each creates essential conditions for the next, or the results of some need to be known to determine the next course of action.

Isolated or Non-Sequential Decisions: These decisions don't create conditions or information necessary for others, so the order in which they are made does not matter.

Not adhering to the order in which sequential decisions must be made results in delays, as time and effort must be spent retracing steps to get back on track.

–"Haste is slow." (Latin Proverb)[125]

–"He who rushes too much ends up late."

–"The fool and the stingy man walk the same path twice." (Spain)[126]

–"He who strays from the path arrives late or not at all." (Chile)[127]

Rushing also leads to failure when the damage caused prevents restarting the process.

–"Forcing evolution is destroying it."

–"If you start the house from the roof, it will collapse."

–"Don't try to begin with the end."

Degree of Knowledge About Possible Consequences

With Certainty: There is sufficient and adequate information about the problems to be solved, so there is clarity regarding the potential outcomes of the alternatives.

With Uncertainty: Decisions are made with little or no information, making it impossible to predict the possible outcomes.

With Risk: The level of information is partial, and the potential outcomes can only be predicted in terms of probabilities. This is an intermediate state between adequate information and uncertainty.

From the Plate to the Mouth, the Soup Can Spill

There's no absolute certainty about the possible outcomes of decisions, not even the simplest ones, which means that every decision, no matter how straightforward, carries a margin of error.

–*"Every gain has its risks."*

–*"In every attempt, there's a risk of failure."*

–"In every battle, a man must carry two sacks: one for winning and one for losing." (Afro-Cuban Saying)[128]

–"Playing and never losing, that can't be." (Spain)[129]

–"Playing and losing, that can happen." (Spain)[130]

The Eyes Are Useless If the Mind Cannot See

Deciding from ignorance is like doing it blindly or playing Russian roulette, leaving everything to chance.

–"The ignorant and the blind walk by feel."

–"Ignorance brings one down in the fight." (Guinea)[131]

–"He who doesn't know is like one who can't see." (Spain)[132]

Sometimes this leads to very undesirable consequences.

–"Whoever ignores what they shouldn't, pays for what they don't want."

–"Knowing little demands much." (Spain)[133]

On the other hand, having an optimal level of information, within the real possibilities of obtaining it and the time available for deciding, reduces uncertainty and allows for more informed decisions.

–"Knowledge is light."

- *"People call knowledge luck." (Spain)*[134]

Effect on Problems

Effective or Adaptive Decisions: These lead to or bring you closer to solving problems and achieving goals.

Ineffective Decisions: These do not solve the problems, leaving them unresolved.

Harmful Decisions: These worsen the problems or move further away from achieving the goals.

The purpose of decisions is to solve problems and achieve the objectives they are aimed at. One of the criteria for evaluating decisions, though not the only one, is their effectiveness in producing the desired or expected result.

– *"Some people know how to hit the nail on the head."*

– *"You must find the key that opens the door."*

Decisions can sometimes leave problems unresolved without making them worse.

– *"You can't fill your stomach by painting bread." (China)*[135]

– *"Promises don't cover the table." (Spain)*[136]

– *"Fantasy after fantasy leaves the belly empty." (Spain)*[137]

With this type of decision, resources are often wasted and time is lost. Remaining with unresolved problems and unmet goals while the world constantly evolves means falling behind.

– *"Not progressing is regressing." (Latin Saying:* Non progredi est regredi*)*[138]

– *"He who stops walking, stays behind." (Chile)*[139]

Other decisions worsen the situation, increasing suffering and frustration.

– *"Sometimes the cure is worse than the disease." (Spain)*[140]

– *"Some people wipe their eyes and end up blinding themselves."*

Some People Stumble Twice on the Same Stone

Sometimes ineffective and harmful decisions are made repeatedly, which perpetuates the problems and the suffering that comes with them.

–*"The man who makes a mistake and doesn't correct it makes another mistake." (Confucius)*[141]

–*"To err is human, but to persist in error is foolish."*

–*"What has one learned from their mistakes if they continue to repeat them?"*

–*"He who stumbles twice on the same stone deserves to break his head." (Spain)*[142]

STAGES OF THE DECISION-MAKING PROCESS

Decision-making, like any process, involves several stages, which will be presented below.

Establishing and Prioritizing Objectives

Objectives Are Points of Focus for Our Will and Energy

Having clarity about what needs to be done and the objectives to be achieved is crucial for making decisions. Without this clarity, one wouldn't know the purpose of their decisions. Moreover, only by having strategic or broader objectives will the intermediate or tactical goals make sense, as they serve as the means to reach the larger goals. Operational objectives define the specific actions required to achieve the tactical ones. Together, they organize decision-making and activity, which is essential for ensuring that decisions are effective.

–*"The lame man gets ahead on the path to his goal, while the one who strays from it does not." (Colombia)*[143]

–*"You reach what you aim for. "*

The Dog Has Four Legs but Can Only Follow One Path (Afro-Cuban Saying)[144]

Even when goals are on the same hierarchical level, achieving some may slow down or exclude the achievement of others.

- *"You can't blow and sip at the same time." (Spain)*[145]

–*"You can't ring the bells and be in the procession." (Spain)*[146]

This is why it's essential to establish a clear order of priorities to choose wisely and organize our actions.

–*"When priorities are clear, decisions become easier."*

A Well-Defined Problem is a Problem Half-Solved

Identifying Problems or Deviations from Objectives

Once goals are set and prioritized, it's essential to identify situations that cause deviations from those goals or problems that require solutions.

–*"Knowing a problem is already more than half of its solution." (José Martí)*[147]

Searching for Options or Alternative Solutions

The next step is to look for possible alternatives or solutions from which one or more must be chosen.

–*"Alternatives are the raw material of decision-making."*

Defining Criteria for Choosing and Assigning Weight to Them

It's important to define or establish the criteria or principles by which these options will be evaluated. These criteria help pre-determine what will be allowed and what won't, allowing part of the decision-making process to be done calmly, rather than under the pressure of circumstances.

Each person has a worldview and moral culture that provides all or part of the references for many decisions, but sometimes problems are new, requiring new criteria to be developed or found.

To Each Their Own (Spain)[148]

How should these criteria be defined? This is a very personal matter since options that are considered very good and desirable for some may not be for others, and neither needs to be wrong.

– *"There's no disputing tastes." (Czech Republic)*[149]

– *"What some despise, others desire." (Spain)*[150]

– *"What one refuses, another begs for." (Spain)*[151]

– *"Bring your goods to market, some will say they're good, others will say they're bad." (Spain)*[152]

Enjoyment Makes the Itch Bearable (Cuba)[153]

There are options that, while unpleasant to many, are highly desirable to some.

- *"He who dies by his own choice even finds the soil good." (Panama)*[154]
- *"He who chooses to be an ox even licks the yoke." (Mexico)*[155]
- *"He who dies by his own choice finds death glorious." (Afro-Cuban Saying)*[156]
- *"He who dies by his own choice finds death as sweet as coconut candy." (Cuba)*[157]
- *"May everyone's preferences fatten them up." (Mexico)*[158]
- *"A load carried with joy feels light." (Spain)*[159]
- *"A pleasing burden is easily borne." (Spain)*[160]
- *"It's not hell if you enjoy the burn."*

Conversely, there are options that may be very appealing to most but are unpleasant for some.

- *"Paradise taken with displeasure is poorly endured."*
- *"Even paradise isn't good if you dislike it."*

While the criteria should align with the decision-maker's convictions and preferences, they should also bring solutions closer to the problems and the achievement of broader strategic goals, generate the greatest possible good for those involved, or at least avoid causing unjustified harm to others and the decision-maker.

–"Do not do to others what you would not want for yourself." (Confucius)[161]

Since each alternative will meet some criteria well and others not as much, it's important to assign weight to these criteria, or in other words, establish a hierarchy.

–"Good things happen when you clarify your priorities."

Deliberation and Choice Among the Options or Solutions

With the problems identified and the possible solutions found, it's time to deliberate and choose the best among them based on the established criteria.

There's No Sky Without Clouds Nor Paradise
Without Serpents

It's common that when examining alternatives, you'll find both positive and negative aspects. These must be considered when choosing between them.

- *"If you want a mule without flaws, you'll have to walk." (Spain)*[162]
- *"Even the best firewood has some ants." (African Saying)*[163]
- *"There's no forest without dry branches." (Romania)*[164]
- *"There's no honey without bitterness." (Spain)*[165]
- *"There are no roses without thorns." (Spain)*[166]

To Arrive, Organize Yourself

Planning to Implement the Chosen Option

After making a decision, it's crucial to define how, when, where, and with whom the selected alternatives will be implemented, as well as the order in which the actions will take place.

–"Action accomplishes; thought organizes action." (Afro-Cuban Saying)[167]

Especially when actions must follow a sequence where some steps prepare the way for others.

–"First build the stable, then buy the cow." (Czechoslovakia)[168]

Implementing the Chosen Option

Decision-making doesn't end with deliberation and planning; it's essential to move from thought to action by implementing the chosen course of conduct.

–"Having the solution in mind but not putting it into practice solves nothing." (Afro-Cuban Saying)[169]

–"Planning is valuable when applied."

–*"He who doesn't carry out his plans doesn't enjoy their benefits." (Afro-Cuban Saying)*[170]

–*"A purpose alone won't break a stone." (Germany)*[171]

Evaluation of Results and Introduction of Corrective Measures

Next, it's important to assess the outcomes of the actions.

–*"If you don't check, how do you know it went well?"*

–*"What's left to the wind, the wind takes away." (San Salvador)*[172]

–*"Work not monitored is money lost."*

–*"He who neglects, mismanages." (Chile)*[173]

Then, corrective measures should be introduced to address any aspects that aren't functioning as expected and that deviate from the desired results.

Life is Like Riding a Bicycle, to Keep Your Balance, You Must Keep Moving

With every decision made and implemented, a person finds themselves in a new situation, with a fresh range of possibilities and the need to make more decisions. This is an ongoing process that requires continuous attention to stay in tune with life's demands.

–*"Either you sail, or you sink." (Spain)*[174]

–*"The shrimp that falls asleep gets swept away by the current." (Mexico)*[175]

–*"A pot that isn't stirred burns." (Mexico)*[176]

~~~

FINAL CONSIDERATIONS

Decision-making is the process by which an individual chooses between two or more alternatives, establishes a course of action, carries it out, verifies the results, and sets corrective measures.

There are many ways to classify decisions, some of which include: Importance, urgency, rationality behind the decision, complexity, reversibility, number of people involved, frequency with which they must be made, level of generalization of the objectives they aim for, presence of established procedures for execution, availability of knowledge and skills to make them, level of emotional commitment to solving the problems, temporal relationship with the problems they solve, sequencing, degree of knowledge about their possible consequences, effects of these decisions on the problems.

The decision-making process consists of the following phases or stages: setting and prioritizing goals, identifying problems or deviations from the goals, searching for options or alternative solutions, defining selection criteria and assigning weight to them, deliberating and choosing between the options or alternatives, planning to implement the chosen option, implementing the decision, evaluating the results and introducing corrective measures.

~~~

Chapter II. DEVIATIONS IN DECISION-MAKING

This chapter highlights the most significant moral vices or negative moral qualities that can appear in each stage of the decision-making process.

MORAL VICES IN EACH STAGE

Establishing and Prioritizing Objectives

If You Don't Know Where You're Going, No Path Will Take You There (Qur'an)[177]

Deviations in this stage are forms of imprudence and can include a lack of goals, insufficient emotional commitment to them, or the presence of unreachable or poorly prioritized goals.

Lack of Goals or Purpose:

Without goals to serve as a desired destination to compare with the current situation and guide efforts, opportunities are missed, and time is wasted due to a lack of direction.

–*"A man without purpose is like a ship without a rudder."*

–"Without goals and plans to reach them, one is like a ship setting sail with no destination."

–"There's no favorable wind for one who doesn't know where they're going."

–"If you don't know where you're going, where will you end up?"

Without objectives, any means become pointless, and success is unattainable.

–"There are no achievements without goals."

–"Means without an end are useless."

This condition often leads to significant discomfort, which can be particularly intense and is incompatible with mental health.

–"A life without purpose is an early death."

–"Not reaching goals causes frustration; having none causes despair."

It may also lead to vices as attempts to alleviate the discomfort caused by this void.

–"He who doesn't know where he's going ends up anywhere."

–"He who throws himself to the wind is carried away by it." (Cuba)[178]

Lack of Emotional Commitment to Goals:

Having goals without emotional commitment can cause dissatisfaction, unhappiness, and even illness.

–"There are things we aren't born for, and if we do them, they undo us." (Afro-Cuban Saying)[179]

This lack of commitment often leads to abandoning the struggle when facing pressure, preventing the persistence necessary to achieve goals.

–"Is it a weakness of will or a weakness of commitment to the goals?"

–"Without passion for the goal, you can achieve good results, but not excellent ones."

–"Nothing great has been accomplished in the world without passion."

Furthermore, it prevents dedicating time to goals to which one is truly committed, and therefore more likely to succeed.

–"He who doesn't follow his path won't find his fortune." (Afro-Cuban Saying)[180]

Unreachable Goals:

Setting unreachable goals leads to disorientation, as there are no effective means or procedures to achieve them. This results in wasted time, resources, and missed opportunities to achieve realistic goals.

–"He who insists on making an impossible dream come true fails." (Afro-Cuban Saying)[181]

Poor Prioritization of Goals:

This can manifest by prioritizing morally questionable goals, dedicating oneself entirely to goals disconnected from reality, or assigning too many goals the same level of importance, even if they are all socially acceptable. It can also occur when goals that should only be seen as means are prioritized as ends.

–"Good decisions can't come from bad priorities."

–"Bad strategy defeats us." (Afro-Cuban Saying)[182]

–"He who makes secondary things primary does wrong." (Spain)[183]

Morally Inappropriate Goals:

Socially unacceptable goals that unjustifiably harm others will eventually bring bad consequences to those who pursue them.

–"He who walks the wrong path will end badly." (Proverbs 10:9)[184]

– *"He who walks bad paths finds sharp thorns." (Spain)*[185]

– *"He who plays with fire will eventually get burned." (Afro-Cuban Saying)*[186]

– *"He who walks in bad steps will slip sooner or later." (Chile)*[187]

When goals are prioritized without regard to reality or the vital demands faced, important goals that require immediate attention are neglected.

– *"If you postpone necessary decisions, you cannot be happy."*

He Who Chases Two Hares Catches None (Czechoslovakia)[188]

When too many goals are placed at the same high level of importance, even if they are all socially acceptable and potentially worth prioritizing, attempting to achieve them all at once often exceeds individual capacity, leading to failure in achieving any of them.

– *"He who tries to grasp too much, holds too little." (Afro-Cuban Saying)*[189]

– *"A greyhound that raises many hares kills none." (Spain)*[190]

–"A greyhound chasing two hares returns with none." (Mexico)[191]

–"A suitor chasing many ends up with none." (Spain)[192]

When Money Isn't a Servant, It's a Master

Finally, some goals work well as means to achieve others, but when they are considered the most important or guiding objectives, they lead to poor decisions. Examples of this are greed and avarice, where instead of earning and saving money to meet needs and improve the quality of life, one lives only to earn and hoard wealth.

– "He doesn't own wealth; wealth owns him." (Franklin)[193]

–"The miser doesn't possess his goods; they possess him." (Spain)[194]

He Who Lives Poor to Die Rich, Call Him a Fool (Mexico)[195]

Due to their senseless hoarding, the miser leaves many important needs unmet, both for themselves and those who depend on them financially.

– *"There's no greed without sorrow." (Spain)*[196]

– *"The miser dies of thirst while standing in the river." (Spain)*[197]

– *"He's a beast, not a person, who doesn't enjoy what he's earned." (Spain)*[198]

– *"If a man is stingy with himself, with whom will he be generous? He takes no pleasure even in his own goods." (Ecclesiasticus 14:5)*[199]

– *"Who drinks vinegar when there's good wine, what wouldn't he do to me?" (Spain)*[200]

– *"The mice in the miser's house are fatter than he is." (African Saying)*[201]

Since these misguided goals monopolize all of a person's activity, they can lead to committing any kind of wrongdoing to achieve them.

–"Vice is a cliff." (Cuba)[202]

–"Vice is the gateway to crime."

There Is No Vice Without Suffering (Spain)[203]

Sooner or later, those who succumb to vice will fall into affliction.

–"Vice forges its own suffering with its own hands."

–"There is no vice without suffering." (Spain)[204]

–"He who is driven by greed without considering the consequences falls into affliction." (Panchatantra)[205]

–"He who gives in to greed ruins his own house." (Proverbs 15:27)[206]

–"There are ways that seem right, but in the end, they lead to death." (Proverbs 14:12-16:25)[207]

Identifying Problems

In this stage, the fundamental deviations are related to ignoring problems that need attention, which prevents one from addressing and organizing to solve them.

–"There's no cure for an unknown illness."[208]

- *"What we don't know, we can't eliminate." (Afro-Cuban Saying)*[209]

This neglect can be due to disorientation, dependence, evasiveness, or procrastination. The disoriented person thinks, but about problems of lesser importance or urgency, neglecting the truly significant ones. This can happen due to a lack of commitment to goals or poor prioritization.

- *"The mind in the marketplace, while the food burns."*
- *"I was staring at the moon and fell into the lagoon." (Spain)*[210]
- *"Listening to stories of birds while letting the child fall from your lap." (Malaysia)*[211]
- *"He who watches the wind won't sow, and he who watches the clouds won't harvest." (Ecclesiastes 11:4)*[212]

The Dependent hands over important life decisions to others that they should make themselves.

- *"Do you know who decides how you should live? - You."*
- *"The responsibility for your life is yours; don't give it to others."*
- *"If you don't make your own decisions, someone else will, and they won't think about your happiness as much as you do."*

Always Trying to Please Everyone Is for Parachutists

Some may decide, but based on other people's criteria or with the intent to please everyone, which ultimately leaves them unhappy with themselves.

–*"An ear that listens to every language confuses its head." (Afro-Cuban Saying)*[213]

–*"If you live for others' opinions, you're already dead."*

–*"Don't betray yourself just to be liked by everyone."*

–*"When you try to please others above all, you end up not pleasing someone very important: yourself."*

–*"Pleasing everyone is not only impossible but absolutely unnecessary."*

Some People Are Like Ostriches, Burying Their Heads in the Sand to Avoid Seeing Things

The evasive or escapist person avoids facing certain decisions because the related problems cause them significant discomfort.

– *"No matter how much we close our eyes, reality doesn't disappear." (Afro-Cuban Saying)*[214]

– *"He who keeps his eyes closed doesn't live in reality." (Afro-Cuban Saying)*[215]

– *"Not wanting to see can't stop time." (Afro-Cuban Saying)*[216]

– *"There's no worse blind person than the one who refuses to see, nor worse deaf person than the one who refuses to hear." (Spain)*[217]

– *"You can evade reality, but not the consequences of evading it."*

– *"Avoiding problems you need to face is avoiding the life you need to live."*

It's common for escapists to hide behind justifications.

– *"He who wants to do something finds a way, he who doesn't, finds excuses."*

– *"For what a man doesn't want to do, he will find an ailment." (Spain)*[218]

– *"He who has no desire finds everything painful." (Czechoslovakia)*[219]

They may blame others and circumstances for their avoidance and the consequences it brings.

– *"If you don't want to fish, don't blame the sea."*

– *"You can't blame the wind for the mess if you left the window open."*

They may even present themselves as victims while evading their own responsibility for their actions and life direction.

– *"Once you can take the wheel of your life, the responsibility is yours."*

– *"Some victims spend their lives seeking out villains to justify their unhappiness."*

– *"If you play the victim, the universe will only give you crumbs."*

The procrastinator, on the other hand, habitually delays tasks or situations that need attention, replacing them with irrelevant or more enjoyable activities.

– *"What's left for later, stays for later."*

– *"The street of 'later' leads to the plaza of 'never.'" (Colombia)*[220]

– *"In delay lies danger." (Chile)*[221]

– *"Don't put off for tomorrow what you should do today."*

Searching for Options or Alternative Solutions

Some People Are in the Town and Don't See the Houses

Once problems are identified, deviations such as narrow-mindedness and confusion may arise, leading to a limited search for alternatives. This results in considering only a small group of options, sometimes rejecting others for unjustified reasons.

- *"Eyes are useless to a blind brain."*
- *"With closed eyes, you cannot move forward." (Afro-Cuban Saying)*[222]
- *"A narrow mind brings one down in the fight."*
- *"Some are in the forest but don't see wood for the fire."*
- *"We can die of thirst with water in front of us, unable to realize it's there."*

Mirages Are Not Reality (Afro-Cuban Saying)[223]

Lack of objectivity can lead to seeing options that don't exist.

–*"He who lives on illusions dies of disappointment." (Afro-Cuban Saying)*[224]

–*"He who lives in dreams is awakened by reality." (Afro-Cuban Saying)*[225]

–*"He who lives his lie is killed by his truth." (Afro-Cuban Saying)*[226]

Naivety and Simplicity:

This arises when someone fails to verify the information they've received or doesn't pay attention to its sources.

–*"The simple believe everything." (Cuba)*[227]

–*"Foolish, stubborn, and poorly advised, he will be a failure." (Afro-Cuban Saying)*[228]

–*"He who lets a rooster lead him will sleep in the henhouse." (Arab Saying)*[229]

When the Blind Lead, Woe to Those Who Follow! (Spain)[230]

Some people even seek advice from those who are deeply disordered in the very areas they are being consulted about, or in closely related matters.

–*"Lost is he who follows the lost." (Mexico)*[231]

–*"He who has no advice for himself can hardly give it to me." (Spain)*[232]

Defining Criteria for Selection and Assigning Weight

Deviations in this phase can also be considered forms of imprudence. These include the absence of criteria for evaluating alternatives, defective criteria that are either unattainable or too low, those linked to paralyzing social inhibitions, or the lack of hierarchy among them.

Absence of Criteria:

Without criteria to evaluate the alternatives, the individual may not know how to make a choice and may experience high levels of tension, depending on how significant the problems are for them.

Unattainable Criteria:

When criteria are unattainable, all options are excluded.

– *"He who seeks flawless options never decides."*

Extremely Low Criteria:

When criteria are set too low, they can lead to decisions that cause avoidable suffering.

– *"He who eats both good and bad eats double, but may end up with indigestion."*

The Hawk Doesn't Ask the Dove for Permission to Hunt

When criteria are linked to unjustified social inhibitions, they can improperly block certain options.

– *"Do not show deference to others at your own expense, and do not be ashamed to your own ruin." (Ecclesiasticus 4:22)*[233]

– *"A timid heart wins no honors." (Czech Republic)*[234]

– *"It's useless to ask a cow, 'Please do me the favor of giving me a glass of milk.'" (United States)*[235]

–"Oysters don't open by persuasion."

When there's no hierarchy or order of priority among criteria, there will be confusion when choosing between mutually exclusive options.

- *"Two captains sink the ship." (Turkey)*[236]
- *"When two kings sail in the same boat, one won't reach the goal." (Afro-Cuban Saying)*[237]
- *"Two kings together cannot rule." (Afro-Cuban Saying)*[238]
- *"Leadership doesn't tolerate a pair." (Spain)*[239]

Deliberation and Choosing Between Solutions

In this phase, common deviations include untimely philosophizing, thoughtlessness, desperation, and *catatimia* (emotional bias). Untimely philosophizing happens when one thinks deeply about real problems but ineffectively, as these reflections don't lead to practical decisions or solutions, resulting in exhaustion without progress.

- *"Nothing is more tiring or useless than thinking without deciding."*
- *"You're looking for five feet on a cat, but it only has four." (Cuba)*[240]

Thoughtlessness occurs when a person rushes to make decisions without properly weighing the pros and cons, often leading to undesirable consequences.

- *"Desire without knowledge is not good; haste makes mistakes." (Proverbs 19:2)*[241]
- *"Haste is the father of failure."*
- *"He who rushes delays or loses."*
- *"Haste is a bad counselor." (Mexico)*[242]
- *"Rushing things and doing them well don't go together." (Mexico)*[243]
- *"What's rushed is either raw or burned." (Mexico)*[244]

–"He who cooks in a hurry eats raw."

–"He who decides suddenly repents suddenly." (Spain)[245]

–"He who promises quickly, fulfills slowly and repents quickly." (Spain)[246]

–"Letters written in haste bring a thousand regrets." (Spain)[247]

Banging Your Head Won't Hollow Out the Wall
(Czech Republic)[248]

Reflection may be present, but it can be flawed due to the distress caused by problems, leading to desperate and ineffective actions in trying to solve them.

–"Shouting won't put out the fire." (Czechoslovakia)[249]

–"He who panics and only cries in the face of disaster increases his pain without escaping it." (Panchatantra)[250]

–"He who despairs in misfortune makes it worse." (India)[251]

–"Desperation remedies nothing."

–"The more you grieve, the greater your loss." (Persian Saying)[252]

–"If you lose your head in tough situations, you'll only make things worse."

Distortion can also arise from intense emotional states that cloud reasoning, known as *catatimia.*

–"Where the heart is king, its orders cannot be disobeyed." (Afro-Cuban Saying)[253]

–"Affection blinds reason." (Spain)[254]

–"Muddy water makes no mirror." (Spain)[255]

–"Don't make permanent decisions based on temporary emotions."

Planning to Implement the Chosen Option

After deliberation and choosing among the alternatives, deviations can include a lack of planning or poor planning. This often happens by failing to consider the necessary order in which problem-solving stages must be addressed, or by inaccurately assessing the resources available and one's own ability to use them.

Lack of Planning Leads to Ruin

When there is no planning and no clear definition of how, when, where, and who will implement the chosen alternatives, disorganization follows. This results in unnecessary losses of time and other resources.

–*"A goal without a plan is just a wish."*

The Cart Doesn't Go Before the Oxen (Afro-Cuban Saying)[256]

Not paying attention to the order in which stages must be completed leads to wasted time and effort in retracing steps to get back on track, assuming there are still opportunities to do so.

–*"Forcing evolution is destroying it."*

–*"You don't eat dinner before breakfast." (Afro-Cuban Saying)*[257]

–*"Don't start building the house from the roof." (Mexico)*[258]

–*"Before running, one crawls and walks." (Afro-Cuban Saying)*[259]

–*"What's done by force is destroyed by force." (Afro-Cuban Saying)*[260]

Undervaluation of Resources and Abilities:

This prevents individuals from fully deploying their potential, making success unlikely when full effort is needed.

–*"Self-confidence doesn't guarantee success, but lacking it guarantees failure."*

–*"Without self-confidence, we are only a fraction of ourselves."*

Overvaluation:

Overconfidence can lead to excessive trust in victory and overreaching, often resulting in failure.

–*"He who doesn't know his limitations overreaches and fails." (Afro-Cuban Saying)*[261]

–*"There's no worse blind man than one who, being blind, believes he can see." (Spain)*[262]

–*"There's no worse blind man than one who thinks he sees everything."*

Implementation of the Chosen Option

After deliberation and planning, deviations can lead to either inactivity or inadequate actions in solving problems. Inactivity is a form of indecision, often caused by timidity, insecurity (expressed as fear of failure), a need for absolute certainty or perfect conditions, fear of change, excessive attachment to the current situation, overindulgence, or procrastination.

With Excessive Modesty, You Won't Eat or Dine

The timid person fails to turn decisions into actions due to unjustified fears and paralyzing social inhibitions, which become obstacles in interacting with others and meeting essential needs that require collaboration.

– *"He who's too shy neither eats nor dines." (Mexico)*[263]

– *"Modesty is of no use to a man in need." (Latin Proverb)*[264]

– *"Brother Modest never became prior." (Spain)*[265]

– *"A timid heart wins no honors."*

– *"No timid soul ever reached great heights."*

Fear of Failure:

This often distracts individuals from the task at hand as they focus on potential outcomes. Not only does this cause paralysis, but when action is taken, it's often lacking in quality, leading to failure. This reinforces the fear of failure and creates a vicious cycle.

– *"The bird doesn't fail by falling in its first attempt at flight but by giving up flying out of fear of falling."*

–*"If you try, there's a chance of losing; but if you don't try, there's no chance of winning."*

Seeking Absolute Certainty:

The pursuit of complete clarity and certainty before acting leads to inaction because these are unattainable, no matter how long one waits.

–*"He who insists on seeing everything with absolute clarity before deciding never decides."*

–*"No matter how much we know, there will always be something we don't." (Afro-Cuban Saying)*[266]

The Myth of Perfect Conditions:

It's equally impossible to wait for perfect circumstances to act.

–*"The perfect moment to start something never comes."*

–*"If you wait for your life to line up perfectly before doing something, you'll wait forever."*

–*"If you don't take a risk today, tomorrow you'll find more excuses not to."*

–*"In seeking the best, we often miss out on the good." (Spain)*[267]

–*"The best is the enemy of the good." (Spain)*[268]

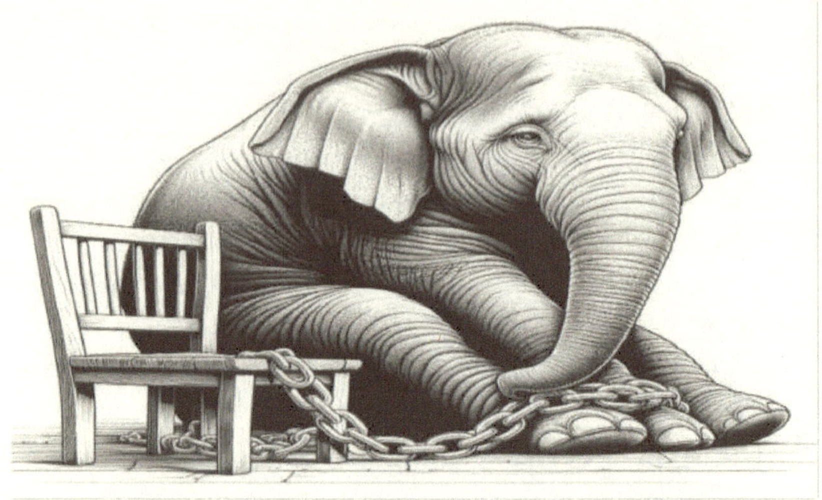

Mental Chains Are Stronger Than Physical Ones

Fear of change often comes with excessive attachment to the current situation, which, though precarious, is familiar and offers some security and advantages. This attachment makes it difficult to decide to change and face the risks inherent in any transition.

–*"As long as inertia and comfort are stronger than the felt need for change, you will stay the same."*

Lack of Action After a Decision:

This can also occur when acting means giving up something one is very fond of, resulting in inaction despite knowing what needs to be done due to a lack of willpower.

–*"There is no greater difficulty than a lack of will." (Spain)*[269]

–*"The weak lack energy in their decisions."*

Procrastination:

This can also arise during the problem-identification phase, where the individual postpones necessary tasks in favor of irrelevant or enjoyable activities.

–*"'Tomorrow' never ends." (Cuba)*[270]

–*"What isn't started, never finishes." (Spain)*[271]

By delaying necessary decisions, problems often grow in difficulty and complexity, making them harder to solve.

–*"No one is more miserable than he for whom indecision has become a habit."*

–*"He who postpones decisions from day to day lives constantly burdened by troubles." (Hesiod)*[272]

–*"A man who hesitates in matters that cannot wait is guilty when fate turns against him and places obstacles in his path." (Panchatantra)*[273]

Inappropriate Actions:

Inappropriate actions in problem-solving may stem from acting without forethought or planning, or from acting at the wrong time despite having planned. This includes impulsivity, haste, and recklessness.

He Who Doesn't Watch Where He Walks Is Likely to Fall (Afro-Cuban Saying)[274]

Acting without forethought leads to action without deliberation or insufficient consideration, essentially skipping from problem identification straight to action, often making the situation worse.

–*"Acting without thinking is like shooting without aiming."*

–*"Acting without thinking can cause us to stumble."*

–*"Quick decisions lead to uncertain results."*

Impulsiveness:

The impulsive person not only fails to think before acting but often doesn't even identify the problems. They act based on their impulses and the impression of the moment, only to regret it later.

–*"Like a city without walls, exposed to danger, is one who cannot control their impulses." (Proverbs 25:28)*[275]

–*"The impulsive act without thinking; the reflective keep their calm." (Proverbs 14:17)*[276]

–*"The fool gives free rein to their impulses, but the wise eventually restrain them." (Proverbs 29:11)*[277]

A Hasty Building Is a Ruinous One

The hurried individual feels pressed for time, which leads to rushed and clumsy actions, often violating the necessary order of execution.

–*"Quick and well almost never go together." (Spain)*[278]

–*"In hurried action, one loses control of oneself." (Lao Tzu)*[279]

–*"Haste is the father of failure."*

He Who Seeks Danger Perishes in It (Panama)[280]

The reckless person exposes themselves to danger without proper reflection, often suffering unnecessary harm.

- *"He who doesn't take care won't meet his grandchildren." (Afro-Cuban Saying)281*
- *"The wife of a careless man almost always ends up a widow." (Hungary)282*
- *"He who exposes himself to useless danger dies a martyr to the devil." (Netherlands)283*
- *"The fish that seeks the hook seeks its doom." (Spain)284*
- *"He who strays from prudent conduct will rest among the dead." (Proverbs 21:16)285*

Evaluating Results and Introducing Corrective Measures

After decisions are carried out, various deviations may appear, such as evasion, excessive and unjust self-blame, weakness, inconsistency, and inflexibility.

Before Trying to Find Someone to Blame, Ask Yourself About Your Own Responsibility

The evasive person avoids acknowledging their share of responsibility for the negative outcomes of their decisions and tries to place the blame on other people or circumstances.

– *"Some create their own storms and then get sad when it rains."*

– *"How can you blame the wind for the mess if you were the one who left the window open?"*

– *"Instead of blaming the drop that overflowed the cup, face the fact that you allowed it to fill up."*

– *"He who willingly seeks trouble shouldn't complain in hell." (Chile)*[286]

From this stance of blaming others, it's common to adopt a victim mentality and self-pity.

– *"If you act like the poor soul, the universe will only send you scraps."*

– *"Keep playing the victim in your drama, and the universe will keep sending you villains."*

Everything That Weighs You Down Isn't Yours to Carry

A deviation opposite to evasion is taking on responsibilities that aren't yours, which often leads to unnecessary guilt, creating a burden that prevents progress.

–*"Some feel they must pay for plates someone else broke."*

–*"Taking responsibility for what is truly yours empowers and allows growth; but guilt, especially undeserved guilt, victimizes and diminishes."*

Both evasion and self-blame serve as distractions that prevent learning from mistakes and building the life you want.

–*"If you avoid your responsibilities or take on those that aren't yours, you won't prosper."*

–*"When you blame others, you give up your power to change."*

–*"Decide to be the protagonist instead of the victim."*

–*"Take responsibility for your life—victims don't succeed."*

Weakness:

This occurs when, despite knowing the decision is right, one gives in to pressure, ultimately harming both others and oneself.

– *"He who relies on the weak will regret it someday."*

– *"He who doesn't take care of himself courts disaster." (China)*[287]

– *"Sometimes our worst enemy is ourselves."*

– *"He who weakens in danger won't earn even what he eats." (Argentina)*[288]

He Whose Spirit Is as Inconsistent as Milk Foam Builds Nothing Lasting in Life (Tuareg Arab Proverb)[289]

The inconsistent person gives up when faced with frustration from not achieving the desired result and abandons the struggle, failing to implement corrective measures.

– *"Without perseverance, talent is barren land." (England)*[290]

– *"Without effort, there is no reward."*

– *"The fool has no fixed goal." (Proverbs 17:24)*[291]

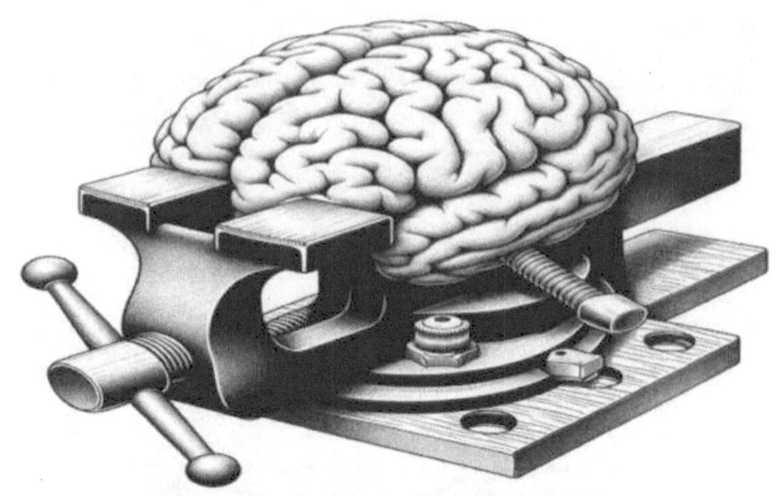

Bad Is the Opinion That Cannot Change

The obstinate and inflexible person holds onto their decisions, even when overwhelming evidence suggests they need to change.

–*"He's not a good bird who gets shot at twice from the same branch."*

–*"Stubbornness leads nowhere." (Afro-Cuban Saying)*[292]

–*"The wise lose their wisdom when they become stubborn." (Afro-Cuban Saying)*[293]

–*"The result of obstinacy is loss." (Afro-Cuban Saying)*[294]

–*"Stubbornness produces loss." (Afro-Cuban Saying)*[295]

–*"The stubborn are destined for much suffering." (Ecclesiasticus 3:27)*[296]

~~~

FINAL CONSIDERATIONS

Among the moral vices that cause deviations at different stages of decision-making are:

Setting and prioritizing goals: Absence or scarcity of goals. Lack of personal commitment to them. Presence of unattainable goals. Insufficient prioritization due to: A. Prioritizing morally questionable goals. B. Devoting oneself entirely to objectives that ignore the demands of the circumstances. C. Having too many goals on the same level of importance, even if they are all socially acceptable. D. Prioritizing some that should only be conceived as means to achieve others. All of the above qualifies as imprudence.

Identifying problems or deviations concerning the goals: Misfocus, where one thinks about less important or urgent problems, neglecting the truly significant ones. Dependence on others for important life decisions that should be made personally. Evasiveness or escapism, avoiding certain decisions because their related problems cause significant discomfort. Procrastination, habitually delaying tasks or situations that should be addressed, replacing them with irrelevant or pleasurable activities.

Searching for options or alternative solutions: Mental narrowness of those who seek alternatives insufficiently, only seeing and considering a small group of them, and even rejecting some for unjustified reasons. Lack of objectivity that leads to seeing options that don't exist. Naivety and simplicity of those who don't verify the information they obtain or pay attention to its sources.

Defining selection criteria and assigning weight to them: Imprudence due to the absence or deficiency of criteria, either because they are unattainable, extremely low, linked to paralyzing social inhibitions, or lacking a clear hierarchy.

Deliberation and choice between options or alternatives: Untimely philosophizing of those who think deeply about problems that require attention but do so ineffectively, leading to no actual decisions. Rashness of those who choose hastily without examining the pros and cons of each option. Poor quality of deliberation when done under intense emotional states that limit reasoning, known as *catathymia*.

Planning to implement the chosen option: Disorganization and lack of planning by those who don't define the circumstances for implementing the selected alternatives or the order of executing actions.

Implementing the chosen option: Indecision of those who fail to translate their decisions into actions due to: A. Paralyzing social inhibitions. B. Fear of failure. C. Insecurity that drives them to seek absolute certainty and perfect conditions, which are impossible to attain. D. Attachment to the comfort of a situation that, though precarious, provides security and some advantages. E. Difficulty in giving up something to which they are greatly attached. Impulsiveness of those who act without reflection, following their first impression or impulses. Hastiness and rashness of those who act under time pressure. Recklessness of those who, knowing the dangers, expose themselves to them irresponsibly.

Evaluation of results and introduction of corrective measures: Evasiveness of those who don't take responsibility for the negative consequences of their decisions and attempt to blame others or external situations. Feeling responsible and guilty for results that were not within their control. Weakness of those who, after acting, yield to pressure in situations where they should remain firm. Inconstancy of those who give up in the face of frustration when they don't immediately achieve the expected results. Stubbornness and inflexibility of those who stick to their decisions despite overwhelming evidence that they need to change them.

~~~

Chapter III. HOW TO MAKE GOOD DECISIONS

This section presents the attitudinal tools and moral qualities necessary for making good decisions.

MORAL QUALITIES NEEDED AT EACH STAGE OF DECISION-MAKING

The circumstances in which a person must make decisions are practically infinite, so the number of moral qualities required is vast. However, a group of key qualities stands out due to their importance and must be considered at each stage of decision-making.

Establishing and Prioritizing Objectives

In this first stage, prudence is essential. It is the ability to guide life toward good objectives through appropriate means. Prudence requires clarity about what one wants and the necessary steps to achieve it.

– *"If you know what you want, you can still make mistakes like anyone else, but you'll make fewer of them."*

When There Are No Dogs, You Hunt with Cats

Objectives must be achievable with the resources at hand.

– *"Happiness comes from using the means you have, not from what's missing."*

– *"Everyone plays with their own cards." (Cuba)*[297]

– *"Each person chews with the teeth they have."*

– *"When there's nothing that works, what doesn't work will do." (Argentina)*[298]

– *"If there's no bread, cakes will do." (Spain)*[299]

– *"If there's no bread, cassava will do." (Cuba)*[300]

– *"If there's no wheat, rye will do." (Spain)*[301]

– *"If you can't do what you want, want what you can." (Spain)*[302]

– *"He who doesn't take what God gives will find misery." (Chile)*[303]

Failing to set realistic goals is a form of disorientation.

– *"If you know you won't reach the goal, don't get involved." (Mexico)*[304]

– *"Don't waste time on what you have good reason to believe won't be achieved." (José Martí)*[305]

– *"It's unwise to pursue what doesn't promise success." (Afro-Cuban Saying)*[306]

– *"Set goals that match your abilities and possibilities." (Afro-Cuban Saying)*[307]

– *"Stretch your legs as far as the blanket reaches." (Afro-Cuban Saying)*[308]

– *"Reach only as far as your hands can go." (Afro-Cuban Saying)*[309]

However, what may seem impossible for most doesn't necessarily mean it is.

– *"When someone tells you a goal is impossible, they're talking about their limitations, not yours."*

– *"People disapprove of what they can't achieve." (Afro-Cuban Saying)*[310]

Many successful people with great goals lacked support from loved ones at first.

– *"Good dreams often seem crazy at the beginning."*

– *"It seems impossible until it's done."*

– *"A person with a new idea is a fool until they succeed."*

– *"The impossible retreats when you advance toward it."*

– *"I didn't know it was impossible, so I did it."*

Goals should bring a sense of usefulness, contributing to the well-being and happiness of others through products or services.

– *"In seeking joy, I realized life is service; when I served, I found joy in service."*[311]

– *"Every man should learn to do something others need." (José Martí)*[312]

Treat Others as You Would Like to Be Treated

At the very least, aim not to cause unjustified harm to others.

–"So in everything, do to others what you would have them do to you." (Matthew 7:12 and Luke 6:31)[313]

–"Hear what virtue is, and ponder it: Never do to others what you would consider bad for yourself." (Panchatantra)[314]

Commitment and Passion:

It's essential that goals reflect your true self and that you have an authentic commitment to them, as this is a cornerstone of success.

–"The moment you commit, the achievement of your goal is almost certain."

–"When you know what you want, and want it enough, you will find ways to achieve it."

Pursuing goals that you are passionate about, which give meaning to your existence, helps you better withstand the pressures that inevitably arise.

–"Nothing tires you if the desire is firm." (Afro-Cuban Saying)[315]

These goals are also the foundation of happiness.

–"Two important dates in your life: the day you were born and the day you found your 'why.'"

–"To beautify life is to give it meaning." (José Martí)[316]

–"If you want to be happy, find goals that guide your thoughts."

–"Only after having a defined purpose in life can we find peace of mind. Only after achieving peace of mind can we enjoy true rest." (Confucius)[317]

Personal Growth:

Pursuing meaningful goals marks a key moment in a person's maturity.

–"A true passion suddenly transforms a boy into a man."

– *"Sometimes, more important than the goals you achieve is what you become while pursuing them."*

These goals keep you alert to opportunities and sharpen your skills to take advantage of them.

– *"He who has a clear goal makes everything work toward it."*

– *"When someone knows what they want, the universe steps aside to let them pass."*

– *"Aim for the end, and the means will follow." (Spain)*[318]

However, passion alone isn't enough. Goals must be well-prioritized to focus on what truly matters.

– *"Often, improving life is simply a matter of changing priorities."*

– *"Don't waste time on what's not worth it; focus on what truly matters."*

Don't Chase Money, Success, or Love. Become the best version of yourself, and they will eventually follow.

To avoid confusion between those things that work well as ultimate goals and those that should only be considered as means:

–*"Chase the vision, not the money, and the money will end up following you."*

–*"The secret isn't to run after the butterflies, but to take care of the garden so they come to you."*

–*"Be the best version of yourself, and the money will end up following you."*

Identification of Problems or Deviations from Objectives

Identifying Problems or Deviations in Relation to Goals

Like with fruits, events must be addressed neither a day before they're ripe nor a day after. (José Martí)[319]

After defining and prioritizing objectives, it's essential to address problems and deviations promptly.

–*"Acting at the right moment is the key to success." (Arab Saying)*[320]

–*"Many desires and hard-to-reach riches are obtained by brave and determined men who know how to seize the right moment." (Panchatantra)*[321]

–*"The wise... in their actions, love finding the right moment." (Lao Tzu)*[322]

A Stitch in Time Saves Nine

By being timely in decision-making, problems can be solved before they become more complex, requiring much more effort and resources, or even exceeding our ability to resolve them.

–*"A timely stitch saves hundreds." (Chile)*[323]

–*"Prevent disorder before it grows." (Lao Tzu)*[324]

–*"The world's difficult problems must be faced while they are still easy; the great problems of the world must be faced while they are still small." (Lao Tzu)*[325]

–*"Fight the difficulty while it is easy; fight the great while it is small." (Lao Tzu)*[326]

–*"What you can do today with little effort, will cost you more tomorrow." (Afro-Cuban Saying)*[327]

Searching for Alternative Solutions

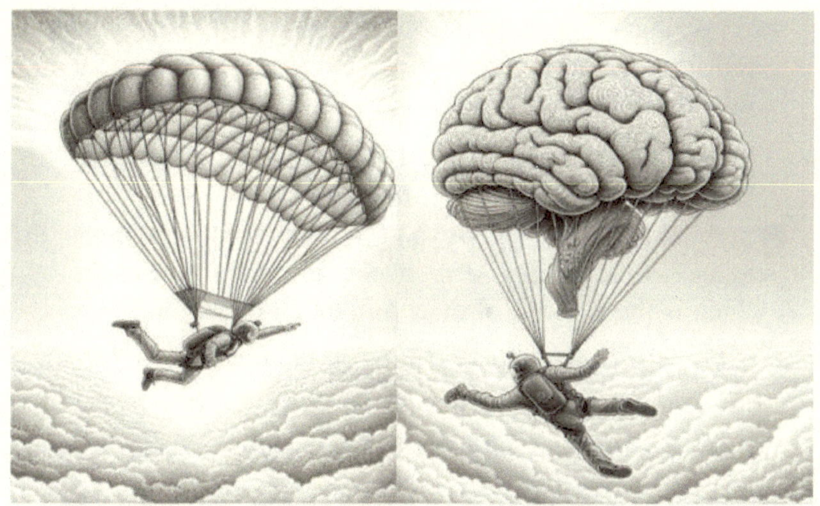

The mind, like a parachute, works best when it's open.

To find effective solutions, an open mind and flexibility are essential.

– *"Keep your mind busy to achieve things; keep your mind open to understand things." (China)*[328]

This openness allows us to consider alternatives that may be difficult to use because they differ from the norm or are somewhat unappealing. However, not using them could be worse.

– *"A compassionate surgeon never made a good cure."*

– *"You have to break the egg before making the omelet." (Spain)*[329]

– *"Some painful procedures are inevitable and even necessary."*

Defining Criteria and Prioritizing Choices

To evaluate alternatives, you need individually crafted and well-founded criteria, which requires a certain degree of authenticity.

–*"Be yourself and try to be happy, but above all, be yourself."*

–*"If you want to be happy, be yourself."*

Establishing a hierarchy and priority order between criteria enables you to choose between mutually exclusive options, which is the essence of discernment and wisdom.

–*"If two ride a horse, one must sit behind."*

–*"Good things happen when you clarify your priorities."*

–*"Give priority to what truly deserves priority."*

A Bird in the Hand Is Worth More Than a Hundred in the Bush (Spain)[330]

Criteria should focus on options that are truly achievable with the resources at hand, which is the essence of **objectivity**.

–*"Adjust your expectations."*

–*"Wars are only won with feet on the ground." (Afro-Cuban Saying)*[331]

–*"Keep your head on your shoulders and your feet on the ground." (Afro-Cuban Saying)*[332]

–*"Don't build castles in the air."*

–*"A sparrow in the hand is better than a hundred geese in flight." (England)*[333]

–*"Stories don't fill bellies." (Galicia, Spain)*[334]

Neither Too Cold to Freeze, Nor Too Hot to Burn

Criteria shouldn't be so high that all options are excluded, nor so low that any option becomes valid.

–*"It's just as bad to overshoot as it is to fall short." (Cuba)*[335]

–*"Neither so high you pass the sky, nor so low you scrape the ground."*

–*"Neither too close to burn, nor too far to freeze." (Chile)*[336]

–*"Not pruning is bad, but over-pruning is worse." (Spain)*[337]

Deliberation and Selection of Alternatives

In this stage, **discernment** is essential to assess and compare options before choosing.

–*"A decision based on reason and intelligence is like plaster on a smooth wall." (Ecclesiasticus 22:17)*[338]

Fish or Cut Bait (United States)[339]

Reflection should focus on key aspects of the problems and truly lead to their resolution, avoiding unnecessary details.

–*"In deliberations, get to the point."*

–*"Don't look for five feet on a cat; it only has four."*

–*"Either sing or be silent." (Spain)*[340]

–*"Take it or leave it." (Spain)*[341]

The Wise Man Only Dwells on His Troubles When It Leads to Practical Solutions

Avoid engaging in unnecessary worries that prevent channeling the discomfort caused by problems in a productive way.

–*"Time shouldn't be wasted on suffering; it should be used to fulfill our duties." (José Martí)342*

–*"Let's think about our problems to find practical solutions, not to torment ourselves."*

–*"Replace the word 'worry' with 'action' in resolving your problems."*

Don't let the inevitable storms of life defeat you.

Don't Do Anything of Importance Without Consulting Your Pillow (Spain)[343]

It's wise to take the necessary time to deliberate, as some elements only become clear after a period of reflection.

–*"To a hasty question, a spacious answer." (Spain)*[344]

– *"To a quick question, a slow answer." (Italy)*[345]

Before Making Monumental Decisions, First, calm yourself.

It's crucial to remain balanced and seek, or wait for, the best mental state to process the information available.

–*"Don't make decisions in moments of despair."*

–*"Don't respond to a letter when you're hungry."*

–*"For decisions: A hot mind and a cold heart."*

–*"Head in the clouds, feet on the ground." (Afro-Cuban Saying)*[346]

Call Bread, Bread and Wine, Wine (Spain)347

This approach **helps** you stay grounded in reality and see things as they truly are, which is **objectivity**.

–*"Call things by their name."*

It's also important to maintain **independence** when making decisions, basing them on your own criteria.

–*"Hear everyone's advice, but follow your own." (Spain)*[348]

–*"The wise make their own decisions, while the ignorant follow public opinion."*

He Who Doesn't Listen to Advice Doesn't Grow Old
(Afro-Cuban Saying)[349]

While it's essential to maintain independence, it's also important to consider the perspectives and information that others can offer.

- *"Have your own ideas. Listen to advice." (Afro-Cuban Saying)*[350]
- *"Turn a deaf ear to foolish words; pay attention to good advice." (Afro-Cuban Saying)*[351]
- *"A head that doesn't listen to reason has no brains." (Chile)*[352]

Planning to Implement the Chosen Option

To carry out the chosen solution, you must organize and clearly define the order in which actions should be taken, considering the different stages of the process.

- *"Between planting and harvesting, there is watering and waiting."*
- *"Do things right the first time, so you don't have to redo them." (Afro-Cuban Saying)*[353]

It's also crucial to specify **how, when, where, and by whom** the solution will be implemented.

– *"The wise... in their actions, love finding the right moment." (Lao Tzu)*[354]

– *"Success lies in timing."*

– *"Things are done at the precise moment." (Afro-Cuban Saying)*[355]

This ensures the **optimal and rational use** of available resources.

– *"Carefully thought-out plans bring good results; hasty ones lead to ruin." (Proverbs 21:5)*[356]

Implementation of the Chosen Option

At this stage, after deliberation and planning, moral qualities are needed to:

–Wait for the right moment to act.

–Begin when the time is right.

–Take necessary precautions to avoid damage or setbacks.

–Maintain commitment despite pressures to give up.

–Withdraw if necessary.

The Majá Doesn't Catch the Hen by Running, but by Watching (Cuba)[357]

Patience helps overcome the discomfort of necessary waiting, making it essential to wait for the right moment to act, which is a key condition for success.

– *"Patience is the key to paradise." (Turkey)*[358]

– *"The world belongs to the patient man." (Italy)*[359]

– *"He who can wait, gets what he wants." (Spain)*[360]

– *"Fortune favors those who know how to wait wisely."*

– *"A moment of patience brings ten years of comfort." (Greece)*[361]

– *"With patience and a hook, even the greenest fruit falls." (Cuba)*[362]

– *"Skill and patience succeed where force fails."*

– *"To conquer, you need patience and cunning."*

Daring helps break the mental inertia that makes taking the first step difficult.

– *"Sometimes, starting is the hardest part of the journey." (Spain)*[363]

–"Every beginning is hard." (Germany)[364]

–"The first step doesn't take you where you want to go, but it gets you out of where you are."

A Task Begun Is Half Done (Spain)[365]

Taking the first step is crucial to completing a task or achieving a goal.

–"No one finishes without having started." (Czechoslovakia)[366]

–"All things need a beginning." (Spain)[367]

–"A task begun with enthusiasm is half done." (Czech Republic)[368]

–"A good beginning is half the work." (Spain)[369]

–"Starting is the beginning of finishing." (Mexico)[370]

–"A journey begun is half concluded." (Mexico)[371]

–"In anything, the beginning is a very important part." (Spain)[372]

Courage is also necessary to face the risks inherent in every decision.

–"Fortune lends a hand to the bold." (Spain)[373]

–"Without daring, there is no glory."

–"Fortune favors the bold." (Audaces fortuna juvat: Virgil)[374]

–"To undertake is to conquer." (Spain)[375]

–"Be bold, and you will be fortunate." (Spain)[376]

Look Before You Leap (England)[377]

Caution helps ensure careful actions and the timely taking of measures to avoid unnecessary and foreseeable harm or inconveniences.

–"It's better to be safe than sorry."

–"Better to prevent than to regret." (Afro-Cuban Saying)[378]

–"Better a 'just in case' than a 'who could've known'." (Spain)[379]

–"He who eats fish should beware of the bones." (Afro-Cuban Saying)[380]

–"A cautious man is worth two."

–"He who climbs a tree should mind his grip." (England)[381]

–"Even if the water is calm, don't believe there are no crocodiles." (Malaysia)[382]

– *"Don't put your hand in a still river." (Spain)*[383]

– *"A second glance costs nothing." (China)*[384]

– *"Think about the exit before entering." (Arab Saying)*[385]

– *"When you don't know the terrain, look before you step." (Afro-Cuban Saying)*[386]

Firmness allows you to stick to your resolutions, despite pressures that may arise.

– *"The best aid in carrying out a project is the firmness of the person who proposes it." (Benjamin Franklin)*[387]

– *"A character should be like marble: white and strong." (José Martí)*[388]

– *"Straighten your heart and remain firm, and don't be troubled in times of misfortune." (Ecclesiasticus 2:2)*[389]

– *"Blessed is the man who endures the test with strength, for when he is approved, he will receive the reward of life." (James 1:12)*[390]

They'll Criticize You for Everything. Just Live.

Among the pressures we need to overcome is the weight of others' opinions.

- *"If a gentleman looks within himself and is certain he has acted well, what has he to fear or worry about?" (Confucius)*[391]
- *"When you are convinced that what you are doing is your duty, don't hide, no matter how unfavorable people's judgments of you and your actions may be. If the action is bad, don't do it. If it is good, why fear those who wrongly condemn you?" (Epictetus)*[392]

Evaluation of Results and Introducing Corrective Measures

After implementing your decision, moral qualities like **constancy**, **flexibility**, and **maturity** are essential to make the necessary adjustments to resolve problems and achieve the desired goals. These traits help you take responsibility for the outcomes of your decisions and continue on the right path.

He Who Perseveres Triumphs, and He Who Sets His Mind Achieves (Afro-Cuban Saying)[393]

Often, goals aren't achieved immediately; instead, progress is made gradually, requiring **monitoring** to guide actions toward the desired outcome. For this, **constancy** is essential.

–*"Constancy is the most reliable support for human ambition."*

–*"Constancy is the root of prosperity." (Panchatantra)*[394]

–*"Good comes to those who have perseverance."*

–*"Perseverance is crowned with success."*

–*"In the end, if you stick with it, you will succeed."*

You Must Be Willing to Abandon False Paths

Flexibility is the key moral quality that allows you to make necessary adjustments for solving problems and achieving your goals.

– *"If you've taken the wrong path, don't feel sorry for yourself; turn around!"*

– *"I decide according to the circumstances of the time and act accordingly." (Confucius)*[395]

– *"Firm in principles, but flexible in approach."*

You Won't Break a Rock with an Egg
(Czechoslovakia)[396]

Changes may be needed in the **means** when they become defective or insufficient.

- *"You can't catch a hippo with a fishing net." (Afro-Cuban Saying)*[397]
- *"A gourd with a hole isn't good for a cup." (Cuba)*[398]
- *"A chair without a seat is no good for sitting." (Afro-Cuban Saying)*[399]
- *"What use is a lamp without a wick?" (Spain)*[400]

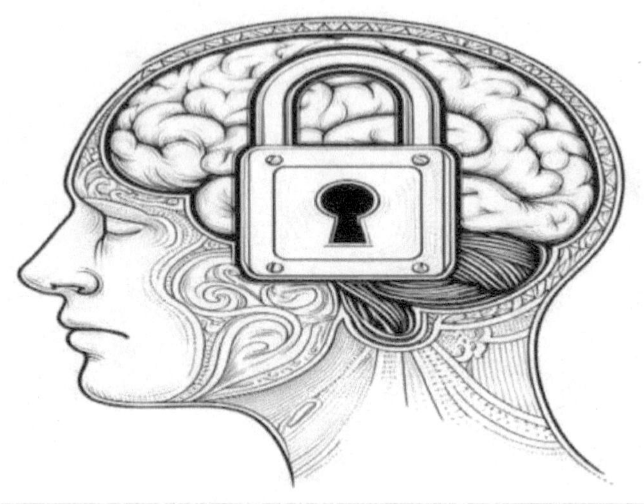

Don't Be Rigid, Focus on the Results

In the **procedures**, it's important to adapt when necessary.

– *"Shouting won't kill the rabbit, even with good aim."*

– *"You can't catch birds just by running after them." (Romania)*[401]

– *"If it doesn't work one way, try the other."* (*Afro-Cuban Saying)*[402]

– *"Don't fear necessary changes."*

Or even reconsider your **goals**, which might demand a price in time and effort that you're not willing to pay.

– *"If you know you're lost, change your counsel and your path."*

– *"Can't catch trout? Gather clams." (Cuba)*[403]

When the Land Won't Yield, Prepare to Move

Sometimes, goals that were once attainable may no longer be, and it becomes necessary to modify or abandon them.

–*"A wise farmer doesn't till land that bears no fruit." (Spain)*[404]

–*"A business that doesn't profit, is best left behind."*

–*"Don't search where there's nothing to find." (Spain)*[405]

–*"If something isn't moving forward, let it go and keep moving yourself."*

It's No Use Crying Over Spilled Milk (England)[406]

Maturity allows us to take responsibility for the consequences of our actions or omissions.

–"What's done is done." (Afro-Cuban Saying)[407]

–"What happened cannot be undone."

–"What's done, face it." (Spain)[408]

–"The past is past, but keep an eye on what remains." (Colombia)[409]

Without unnecessary excuses or guilt that doesn't belong to us.

–"When you let go of excuses, you'll find results."

–"You can have results or excuses, but not both."

–"When you truly want something, you'll find a way; the rest are excuses."

–"Those who want to change find means, those who don't find justifications."

Maturity also helps us take steps to minimize losses and move forward.

–"Men are measured by their ability to rise again." (José Martí)[410]

–*"If you fall seven times, get up eight."*

–*"Falling is optional, getting up is mandatory."*

~~~

FINAL CONSIDERATIONS

For each stage of decision-making, there are moral qualities that enable satisfying outcomes, including:

Establishment and prioritization of objectives: Presence of objectives with the following characteristics: A. Achievable. B. Contributing to the well-being and happiness of others, thereby enhancing the sense of usefulness. C. Not causing unjustified harm to others. D. Having a high emotional commitment to them. E. Being properly prioritized. All of the above are part of prudence.

Identification of problems and deviations from objectives: Timeliness in addressing problems based on their importance and urgency.

Search for alternative solutions: Flexibility to see and find alternatives, including those that are different or contrary to the usual ones. Though they may be somewhat unpleasant, it is worse not to use them.

Definition of selection criteria and their prioritization: Authenticity of having individually developed and well-founded criteria. Discernment and wisdom in establishing a hierarchy and prioritization among these criteria to choose between mutually exclusive options. Objectivity in referring to options that are realistically achievable with the available resources.

Deliberation and choice among options or solutions: Discernment in evaluating and comparing options before making a choice. Focusing reflections on key aspects of the problems and their solutions. Equanimity to seek or wait for the best mental state possible to process the obtained information. Objectivity to evaluate reality and options based on facts. Independence to make decisions based on one's own criteria.

Planning to implement the chosen option: Organization in clearly defining the circumstances for implementing selected alternatives or the order in which actions should be executed.

Implementation of the chosen option: Patience to wait for the appropriate moment to act. Boldness in facing necessary risks. Caution to act carefully and take timely measures to avoid potential damage. Firmness in maintaining resolutions despite internal and external pressures, under the right circumstances and in the appropriate manner.

Evaluation of results and implementation of corrective measures: Maturity to assume responsibility for the consequences of decisions made. Perseverance to persist when results are not entirely satisfactory and to steer actions toward the desired outcomes. Flexibility to make necessary adjustments in line with achieving proposed objectives and solving problems.

~~~

GENERAL RECOMMENDATIONS FOR MAKING GOOD DECISIONS

In this section, we go over the main ideas presented in the work. Each idea is offered as a suggestion or exhortation, explained concisely, and followed by a saying, proverb, or quote. This serves as a guide, but keep in mind that the specifics of any decision depend on each individual in their unique situation, which is one of a kind.

1- Make sure you are clear about what you want and what makes you happy. Knowing what you want to achieve and what makes you happy is crucial in decision-making since decisions are typically oriented toward these. They function, or should function, as criteria or patterns for making choices. Without them, you would feel lost. *"He who doesn't know where he's going will end up anywhere."*

2- Set achievable goals. Goals must be possible to achieve with the resources you have or can obtain, as unattainable goals only lead to frustration and stagnation. *"If you know you won't reach the goal, don't get started."*

3- Prioritize your goals. Often, achieving certain goals can slow down or prevent the achievement of others, so it's necessary to set priorities among them. This prevents the frustration and unease caused by goals that won't be reached. *"You can't blow and sip at the same time."*

4- Identify problems or deviations related to your well-being and goals. These deviations are the demands that life constantly presents, requiring decisions that solve them. Ignoring them doesn't make them disappear; in fact, they usually grow and become harder to resolve. *"Identifying a problem is an important part of solving it."*

5- Seek the information you need to see and assess your options. Some decisions are too important to be taken lightly, and without the necessary information, it's like making a decision blindfolded. Achieving satisfactory results in such conditions would be mere luck. *"Without a continuous flow of information, there is no direction."*

6- Take the necessary time to deliberate. Often, after decisions made too quickly, key elements that were not considered emerge. If circumstances allow, it's best to take the time needed to weigh the advantages and disadvantages of each option. *"Those who decide quickly, repent slowly."*

7- To deliberate properly, calm yourself first. Intense emotional states like fear, anger, frustration, and even love or joy can cloud your thinking, leading to decisions you may regret. It's wise to take time to calm down before making rational decisions. *"Avoid making permanent decisions based on temporary emotions."*

8- Address problems promptly, according to their importance and urgency. Acting in a timely manner solves problems before they become more complex, requiring much more effort and resources to resolve—or even surpassing our ability to solve them. *"A stitch in time saves nine."*

9- Look for the right time to act, but don't aim for absolute certainty or perfect circumstances. Since absolute certainty is impossible and perfect circumstances don't exist, waiting for them can cause paralysis. Gather the essential information and ensure the basic conditions are met; from there, you're ready to act. *"If you try to see everything clearly before deciding, you'll never decide."*

10- Listen to advice from many, but follow your own. What works for one person may not work for another. Good decisions are tailored to the individual, and everyone has their own interests—sometimes contrary to yours—that will influence their advice. *"Before asking someone for advice, understand their interests."*

11- Think before you act. Another way of acting blindly is to act without the necessary caution and consideration. Acting in this way will inevitably lead to problems that could have been easily avoided. *"Acting blindly can make everything more complicated."*

12- Dare to take the first step. Decisions are not complete until action is taken. Taking that first step often requires overcoming mental inertia, but it's essential. *"He who doesn't dare, doesn't cross the sea."*

13- If the decision is good, stick to it. Many decisions will face external and internal pressures that could lead you to give up. If you believe the decision is productive and fair, stand your ground. *"The ability to resist temptation reveals true character."*

14- Don't hesitate to change when necessary. If there is enough evidence that the decision is unproductive, or if changing circumstances make it no longer necessary, don't hesitate to adjust it. *"A business that doesn't yield should be let go."*

~~~

GLOSSARY OF TERMS

In this section, six glossaries are presented containing key terms used in the work and other related ones that will help to better understand the topic at hand.

DECISION THEORY

In this compilation, terms related to the decision-making process, its stages, classification, and the criteria for evaluating them are presented.

Affordability: Options that the environment offers to the individual.

Algorithm: A prescribed set of well-defined, ordered, and finite instructions or rules that allows carrying out an activity through successive steps that do not generate doubts for whoever must execute them.

Alternative: The possibility of choosing between several options.

Ambiguity: The quality of being open to more than one interpretation, which can create challenges in decision-making due to unclear or incomplete information.

Analysis paralysis or rational ignorance: An error where a decision is not made because one is excessively and unproductively immersed in the stages prior to implementing the chosen option, often driven by the pursuit of unreachable perfection.

Analysis paralysis: The overthinking or excessive analysis of a situation, leading to an inability to make a decision or take action.

Autonomy: The presence of abilities to decide and opportunities within the social environment to do so.

Bias: A tendency or inclination that affects judgment, often leading to decisions that deviate from objective or rational choices.

Bounded rationality theory: The idea that humans make decisions that are partially irrational due to cognitive limitations, as well as limits in available information and time to process it.

Bounded rationality: A concept that suggests humans make decisions within the limitations of the information they have, cognitive limitations, and time constraints.

Certainty: Knowledge that, due to the confidence in its validity, provides some degree of security in predicting certain future events.

Choice architecture: The way choices are presented to individuals, influencing the decisions they make without restricting their freedom to choose.

Choice: The selection of one alternative from those available.

Cognitive bias: A deviation in mental processing or reasoning that leads to inaccurate judgments and a distorted view of reality.

Cognitive dissonance: The psychological discomfort experienced when holding two conflicting beliefs or when behavior and beliefs do not align, often affecting decision-making processes.

Commitment: The emotional and psychological dedication to a chosen course of action or goal, essential for consistent decision-making and follow-through.

Criterion: A rule applied to make a decision or determine a truth.

Decision classification: Ways to classify decisions based on criteria such as importance, immediacy, rationality, complexity, reversibility, the number of participants, frequency, generalization level of objectives, and the presence of established procedures.

Decision fatigue: The deteriorating quality of decisions made by an individual after a long session of decision-making, leading to less effective choices.

Decision stages: The periods into which the decision-making process is divided, including: 1- Setting and prioritizing goals. 2- Identifying problems and deviations related to objectives. 3- Searching for alternative solutions. 4- Defining selection criteria and assigning weight. 5- Deliberating and choosing between alternatives. 6- Planning the implementation of the chosen option. 7- Action or implementation. 8- Evaluating results and introducing corrective measures.

Decision theory: An interdisciplinary field dedicated to the study of decisions regarding: 1- Describing the psychological phenomena and conditions under which decisions are made. 2- Prescribing or standardizing how decisions should be made and which are the best. 3- Studying the theories used to address the decision-making phenomenon. 4- Applying this theory to specific areas of human development.

Decision tree: A tool to help make relatively complex sequential decisions through the definition of an algorithm.

Decision-making criteria: Rules or standards for classifying alternatives or options in order of convenience.

Decision-making needs: The need to make certain decisions to solve problems, achieve objectives, or for personal growth.

Decision-making: The process by which an individual chooses between two or more possible alternatives, establishes a course of action, implements it, verifies its results, and establishes corrective measures.

Default option: A set of options one ends up with if no decision is made regarding them. Similar to the default settings of software; unless the user changes them, they will work with this configuration. There is a tendency to accept these types of options.

Deliberation: The process by which an individual carefully considers the advantages and disadvantages of the reasons and alternatives of a decision before adopting it.

Diagnosis: An organized procedure to understand something based on concrete data.

Effectiveness: The ability to achieve goals or to achieve the desired or expected effect.

Efficiency: Achieving objectives with a rational use of available resources and thus with a positive cost-benefit ratio.

Ethically correct decision: A decision that was effective in solving problems, had a positive cost-benefit ratio, was made based on the preferences, criteria, and principles of the decision-maker, and its results did not cause unjustified harm to others or the decision-maker.

Goal: The mental anticipation of a result toward which activity is directed, regulating and guiding it.

Heteronomy: The absence of abilities and possibilities in the social environment for the free exercise of one's will.

Heuristics: General and somewhat undefined rules that serve as "mental shortcuts" to solve problems that would be extremely complex step by step. They are useful by reducing cognitive overload and allowing less effort in problem-solving but can lead to cognitive biases.

Illusion of autonomy: Ineffectiveness of options to solve problems or meet needs.

Inadequate prioritization: Preferring reasons, actions, or objectives of little importance under current circumstances and neglecting or insufficiently addressing those that demand attention.

Information: Data with meaning about objects, processes, or phenomena that reduce uncertainty and allow organizing thoughts to make decisions.

Means: Anything that makes it possible to achieve an end, carry out a purpose, or complete a project.

Method: An organized way of proceeding to achieve an objective.

Moment: Opportunity or favorable occasion.

Multistage solution: A response to a problem that must be carried out in a specific order of stages, where some are a necessary preparation for the next.

Negative feedback: A process of comparing the current situation, resulting from the decisions made, with the ideal situation defined or anticipated by the proposed objectives.

Nudge: Small, easy, and economical changes in the environment aimed at altering people's behavior predictably, without prohibiting any options or significantly changing their incentives. Example: Placing fruit at eye level counts as a nudge; banning junk food does not.

Obstacle: An impediment, difficulty, or inconvenience to achieving a goal or satisfying a need.

Opportunity: A chance offered to carry out or achieve something.

Option: A set of possibilities for choice.

Phase: Each of the successive states of a phenomenon.

Planning: A methodical process by which goals are set, the most appropriate means are chosen, and timelines for achieving them are defined before taking action. Through this process, it is decided in advance what needs to be done, who has to do it, how, and when it should be done.

Prediction: A declaration of what will happen under certain conditions.

Prioritizable objectives: Objectives that, given the circumstances and preferences of the decision-maker, should be considered the most important to achieve.

Priority: Subjectively, it is the preference of certain reasons, actions, or objectives over others; objectively, it refers to what is more important and therefore requires the most attention.

Problem: A situation or issue proposed to find a solution.

Risk: The probability of suffering a specific harm if one is under certain conditions or adopts a certain course of action.

Sequence: A set of operations or stages of a process ordered in such a way that each determines the next.

Sequencing: The action and effect of ordering stages in a specific succession where each determines the next or specifying the existing succession between them.

Solution: The answer to a problem.

Stage: A period into which the development of a process is divided.

Strategy: A set of more general objectives that guide and give meaning to the activity and existence of the individual or group.

Tactic: A system of intermediate objectives to achieve strategic goals.

Uncertainty: A state of doubt and insecurity due to a lack of information or little confidence in the information at hand.

~~~

PSYCHOLOGY OF DECISION-MAKING

The terms presented here help to understand why certain decisions are made, what motives sustain them, what mental states are best for making decisions, and which ones can undermine their quality.

Affectivity: A psychological phenomenon expressed through moods, emotions, feelings, and passions, reflecting the quality of experiences in relation to biological and social needs.

Catathymia: Distortion of subjective reality reflection due to emotional influences.

Cognitive Dissonance: The mental discomfort experienced when holding two conflicting beliefs, values, or attitudes, often motivating an individual to reduce this inconsistency.

Decision Fatigue: The mental exhaustion that results from making too many decisions over a short period, leading to reduced decision-making quality.

Despair: A state of mind where hope fades as desired outcomes seem impossible to achieve.

Despondency: A disheartening emotional state characterized by pessimism and a decrease in mood and initiative.

Emotional Intelligence: The ability to recognize, understand, and manage emotions in oneself and others, playing a crucial role in making sound decisions.

Emotional Resilience: The ability to recover quickly from emotional setbacks or challenges, maintaining a balanced state of mind.

Ethical-Moral Sense of Life: A life purpose that contributes to both personal growth and the well-being of others without causing unjustified harm.

Fear: A necessary emotional state for adaptation and survival, experienced as unease or insecurity when danger is perceived, whether real or imagined.

Frustration: A psychological state that arises when goal-directed behavior is blocked by an obstacle, real or imagined, with the intensity of frustration often proportional to the need's importance.

Happiness: A transitory state of well-being and life satisfaction that occurs when one achieves goals related to their sense of purpose.

Hatred: Strong dislike and aversion towards something or someone, often accompanied by the desire for harm.

Hierarchy of Motives: The organization of personal motives based on their ability to drive an individual's activity.

Hope: A state of mind where the desired outcome seems possible.

Impulse: A sudden desire or drive that leads to action without prior reflection.

Intelligence: The ability to solve new situations and adapt effectively to changing circumstances.

Joy: A pleasant emotional state characterized by satisfaction or well-being, often in response to success or achievement.

Love: A feeling of affection and dedication toward someone or something that naturally attracts, completes, and energizes us for living, communicating, and creating.

Motive: The reason behind a person's actions, serving as the foundation and subjective meaning behind their goal-oriented behavior.

Need: The perception of lack and the psychological tension that prompts an individual to seek solutions.

Pain: An emotional tone that often indicates a hostile or unfavorable situation that hinders the satisfaction of certain needs.

Pleasure: A psychological state of well-being resulting from the fulfillment of a need.

Preference: The primacy or advantage one thing holds over another in terms of value, merit, or personal inclination.

Sadness: An unpleasant emotional state characterized by discomfort and dissatisfaction, often triggered by loss or failure.

Self-Control: The capacity to regulate emotions, thoughts, and behaviors, especially in the face of temptations and impulses.

Sense of Purpose: A system of goals that justify an individual's existence as seen from their own perspective, structured around motives occupying the highest positions in the motivational hierarchy.

Serenity: A state of mental calmness and peace, free from any type of disturbance.

Temptation: A stimulus that arouses the desire for something.

Willpower: The conscious desire that leads a person to perform certain actions, with a clear focus on overcoming internal and external obstacles to achieve goals.

~~~

GAME THEORY

This compilation guides the reader on decisions made in interaction with others, who are also making their own decisions to achieve certain objectives, either cooperatively or not.

Backward Induction: A process of reasoning backward from the end of a problem to determine an optimal sequence of actions.

Coalition: A group of individuals or players that make joint decisions to mutually benefit as a system in a particular game.

Cooperative Game: A game in which players coordinate and collaborate to achieve a common goal, winning or losing as a group rather than as individuals.

Decisive Game (Strong Dual Game): A game where the complement of every winning coalition is a losing one, and vice versa.

Dominant Strategy: A strategy that results in the highest payoff for a player, regardless of the strategies chosen by other players.

Game Theory (Also known as Interactive Decision Theory): The study of decisions and behaviors of individuals who interact, cooperatively or not, to achieve certain objectives.

Game: A recreational activity governed by rules.

Iterated Prisoner's Dilemma: A situation where repeated plays offer each player the opportunity to punish the other for non-cooperation in previous games. This can lead to cooperation due to the threat of punishment overcoming the incentive to betray.

Lose-Lose Situation (No-Win Situation): A game in which, no matter the final result, no player benefits.

Mixed Strategy: A situation in which a player randomizes over two or more possible actions based on assigned probabilities, instead of sticking to a single pure strategy.

Multiplayer Game: A game played by several players who may be individual opponents, grouped in teams, or part of one team against the game.

Nash Equilibrium: A situation where all players have implemented strategies that maximize their individual gains, though this may not result in the best outcome for all participants. Better results could be achieved through coordinated efforts.

Non-Cooperative Game: A game where players make decisions independently, seeking personal gain, though their choices may still benefit all players in some cases.

Pareto Efficiency: A situation where no player can be made better off without making at least one other player worse off. It is often considered a desirable outcome in cooperative games.

Payoff Matrix: A table that describes the payoffs in a strategic game for each possible combination of strategies played by the participants.

Payoff: The reward or outcome that a player receives after a decision is made, based on their strategy and the strategies of others.

Player: A participant in a game.

Prisoner's Dilemma: A scenario where two individuals may not cooperate and may even betray each other, despite mutual cooperation leading to a more beneficial outcome for both.

Risk Dominance: A strategy that is safer because it provides a higher payoff in the worst-case scenario compared to other strategies.

Rules of the Game: Guidelines for behavior that individuals must follow, whether cooperatively or not, in order to achieve specific objectives.

Saddle Point: A situation in a game where the minimum payoff of the row (chosen by one player) and the maximum payoff of the column (chosen by another player) are equal, representing an optimal decision for both players.

Simple Game: A game with straightforward rules, involving a finite set of players or coalitions.

Strategy: A plan of action designed to achieve a long-term or overall aim in the game. Players choose their strategies based on the possible actions of others.

Symmetric Game: A game where exchanging the identities of the players does not change the outcomes, as the rewards depend only on the strategies used, not on who plays them.

Tit-for-Tat Strategy: A strategy in iterated games where a player mimics the actions of the other player from the previous round. This can lead to cooperation or retaliation depending on the other player's behavior.

Unbeatable Scenario: A situation where, regardless of the decision made, the outcome is always unfavorable.

Utility: The measure of satisfaction or benefit a player receives from the outcome of a game.

Win-Win Game (No-Loser Game): A game designed so that all participants can benefit in some way, making it advantageous for everyone involved.

Zero-Sum Game: A game where whatever one player gains is exactly what another player loses, so all gains are balanced by losses.

~~~

MORAL QUALITIES AND DECISION-MAKING

In this brief compilation, moral qualities necessary for each stage of the decision-making process to be successfully carried out are presented, along with their corresponding deviations.

Accountability: The obligation to accept responsibility for one's actions and their outcomes, crucial for ethical decision-making.

Adaptability: The ability to modify decisions and reorient efforts based on changing external or internal conditions.

Assertiveness: The ability to express one's opinions and make decisions confidently while respecting the rights and opinions of others.

Boldness: The quality of acting with daring, taking risks, or showing a lack of restraint in behavior.

Caution: The quality of acting with careful consideration and taking appropriate precautions.

Clarity of Purpose: The quality of having a well-defined goal or vision, guiding all decisions toward a clear objective.

Collaboration: The ability to work effectively with others in decision-making processes, fostering cooperative and inclusive solutions.

Courage: The ability to overcome fear and take action in the appropriate time and manner.

Cowardice: The inability to overcome fear in the necessary circumstances and form.

Dependence: A state where one leaves important decisions in the hands of others, showing a lack of personal autonomy.

Determination: The resolve and boldness to make decisions and maintain them once made.

Discernment: The ability to differentiate between things and understand what is right or appropriate.

Discipline: The ability to maintain focus and follow through with decisions despite distractions or challenges.

Empathy: Understanding the feelings and perspectives of others, which aids in making compassionate and just decisions.

Escapism: The tendency to avoid or flee from problems or conflicts that should be faced.

Evasiveness: The habit of avoiding responsibilities, difficulties, or decisions that need to be confronted.

False Confidence: A misplaced belief in one's abilities and resources to achieve goals.

Flexibility: The ability to adapt plans and decisions in response to new circumstances, ensuring ongoing progress toward goals.

Focus: The ability to concentrate on what is important, avoiding distractions that can derail decision-making.

Foresight: The ability to anticipate future consequences of current decisions, helping in planning and long-term goal setting.

Fortitude: The strength to maintain resolutions despite internal and external pressures.

Generosity: The willingness to share time, resources, or support, often influencing decisions that benefit others.

Gratitude: The ability to recognize and appreciate the contributions of others, influencing decisions that promote mutual benefit and cooperation.

Greatness: Moral excellence and the ability to act with a noble spirit.

Haste: The need or desire to perform something urgently without adequate reflection or preparation.

Humility: The recognition of one's limitations and openness to learning from others, which fosters balanced decision-making.

Immaturity: A state where one has not developed sufficiently to make decisions appropriate for their life stage.

Impatience: The inability to endure the discomforts or demands of a necessary wait.

Imprudence: The tendency to act without considering risks or dangers, showing a lack of discernment.

Impulsiveness: Acting or speaking without reflection or restraint, driven by momentary impressions.

Indecision: The difficulty of making a decision or commitment.

Independence: The quality of being self-reliant and making decisions based on one's own criteria.

Indifference: A lack of determination or decisiveness about something important.

Indulgence: Recklessly giving in to one's own inclinations or desires without restraint.

Inflexibility: The inability to change or adapt one's thoughts, feelings, or behaviors when necessary.

Inopportunity: Acting or speaking at the wrong time or place.
Lack of Self-Confidence: A belief that one lacks the resources or abilities needed to achieve goals.

Integrity: The quality of possessing all the necessary moral qualities.

Irrationality: Engaging in behavior or speech that lacks reasonable or thoughtful consideration.

Lack of Self-Control: Difficulty or inability to abstain from something one deeply desires but knows should not be done.

Misplaced Priorities: The habit of focusing on unimportant matters instead of addressing issues requiring immediate attention.

Moral Courage: The capacity to face difficult or unfavorable situations with bravery and conviction.

Objective Thinking: The ability to assess situations dispassionately, based on facts and reality.

Obstinacy: Refusing to change plans or objectives despite evidence of their failure or inadequacy.

Patience: The capacity to endure delays or obstacles without frustration, essential for waiting for the right moment to act.

Perseverance: Firmness and perseverance in resolutions and purposes.

Perseverance: The steadfast pursuit of goals despite obstacles, failures, or discouragement.

Philosophical Overthinking: A tendency to engage in deep theoretical thinking about a problem without reaching practical solutions.

Preparation: The quality of anticipating needs and planning actions in advance to achieve success.

Procrastination: The habitual delay of important tasks in favor of more pleasant or less relevant activities.

Prudence: The ability to deliberate wisely and make sound decisions in difficult situations, guiding life toward good ends through good means.

Quixotism: Idealism to an excessive degree, often disregarding practical realities.

Rationality: Acting in accordance with reason and logic.

Recklessness: Acting without reflection or caution in matters requiring careful thought.

Resilience: The ability to recover from setbacks and continue toward goals, an essential trait in achieving success.

Resolve: The determination and speed with which one carries out decisions once they are made.

Respect: Acknowledging the worth and contributions of others, ensuring that decisions take into account the well-being and dignity of all involved.

Responsibility: The quality of taking care in matters that require attention and accepting the consequences of actions.

Rigidity: Difficulty in modifying ideas or decisions when necessary.

Self-Assurance: Confidence in one's resources and abilities to reach goals.

Selfishness: The tendency to prioritize one's own interests above all else, disregarding the well-being of others.

Short-Sightedness: Acting or thinking without considering long-term consequences or goals.

Strategic Thinking: The ability to plan ahead and make decisions that align with long-term objectives while considering multiple outcomes.

Stubbornness: Persistence in maintaining an error or a mistaken belief despite evidence to the contrary.

Stubbornness: The inability to change one's mind or behavior when necessary.

Superficiality: Acting or speaking in ways that lack depth or careful thought.

Timidity: A shy or inhibited state of being, often characterized by a reluctance to take bold actions or make decisions.

Tolerance: The capacity to accept and respect differences, which can promote harmony in group decision-making.

Trustworthiness: The ability to be relied upon to make fair and honest decisions, earning the confidence of others.

Weakness: The lack of energy or determination in decisions due to an inability to overcome external pressures or personal inclinations.

~~~

BIBLIOGRAPHIC REFERENCES AND NOTES

1. Thucydides. History of the Peloponnesian War. Translated and annotated by Diego Gracián. Preliminary study by Edmundo O'Gorman. Mexico: Editorial Porrúa; 1998.

2. Machiavelli, Niccolò. The Prince. 3rd Edition. Barcelona: Editorial Vosgos SA.; 1975.

3. Pascal, Blaise. Thoughts. Translated and expanded by Xavier Zubiri. Spain: Alianza Editorial; 2004.

4. Simon, Herbert Alexander. Models of Man: Social and Rational; Mathematical Essays on Rational Human Behavior in Society Setting. United States. New York: Editorial Wiley; 1957.

5. Nash, John Forbes. Non-Cooperative Games. Annals of Mathematics, Vol. 54; 1951. pp. 286–295.

6. Schwartz, Barry. The Paradox of Choice: Why More Is Less. USA: Harper Perennial; 2005.

7. Thaler, Richard H., Sunstein, Cass R. Nudge: Improving Decisions About Health, Wealth, and Happiness. USA: Yale University Press; 2008.

8. Heath, Chip, Heath, Dan. Decisive: How to Make Better Choices in Life and Work. Editorial Gestión 2000; 2014.

9. Kahneman, Daniel. Thinking, Fast and Slow. Translated by Joaquín Chamorro Mielke. Barcelona, Spain: Editorial Debate; 2012.

10. Kahneman, Daniel, Siony, Olivier, Sunstein, Cass R. Noise: A Flaw in Human Judgment. Publisher Little, Brown and Company; 2021.

11. Linero Gómez, Alberto. The Power of Decisions. Colombia: Editorial Planeta; 2014.

12. Alecoy, Tirso Jose. Decision Making Linked to Logical Reasoning and Personality. USA: Publisher Smashwords, Inc.; 2019.

13. Corona-Martínez, Luis Alberto. The General Theory of Decision Making and Its Application to the Field of Medical Assistance (I). Medisur [online journal]. 2007 [cited 2022 Mar 1]; 2(1):[approx. 6 p.]. http://www.medisur.sld.cu/index.php/medisur/article/view/43

14. Corona-Martínez, Luis Alberto. The General Theory of Decision Making and Its Application to the Field of Medical Assistance (II). Medisur [online journal]. 2007 [cited 2022 Mar 1]; 2(1): [approx. 5 p.]. http://www.medisur.sld.cu/index.php/medisur/article/view/42

15. Corona-Martínez, Luis Alberto. The General Theory of Decision Making and Its Application to the Field of Medical Assistance (III). Medisur [online journal]. 2007 [cited 2022 Mar 1]; 2(2):[approx. 5 p.]. http://www.medisur.sld.cu/index.php/medisur/article/view/55

16. D'Angelo Hernández, Ovidio. Life Project and Comprehensive Human Development. Revista Crecemos. - Year 6 No. 1 and 2-Puerto Rico and CD of the Event Hóminis'02-La Habana, Cuba. http://biblioteca.clacso.edu.ar/Cuba/cips/20150429033758/07D050.pdf

17. Aristotle. Nicomachean Ethics and Politics. Mexico: Editorial Porrúa, S.A.; 1992.

18. Plato. Dialogues. Complete work in 9 volumes. Madrid, Spain: Editorial Gredos; 2003.

19. Seneca, Lucius Annaeus. On the Shortness of Life, Leisure, and Happiness. Barcelona, Spain: Editorial Acantilado; 2013.

20. Xenophon. Memorabilia; Oeconomicus; Symposium; Apology of Socrates. Madrid, Spain: Editorial Gredos; 1993.

21. Frondizi, Risieri. What Are Values? An Introduction to Axiology. Mexico: Fondo de Cultura Económica; 2009.

22. Fabelo Corzo, José Ramón. Values and Their Current Challenges. Havana: Editorial José Martí; 2011.

23. Báxter Pérez, Esther. When and How to Educate in Values? Havana, Cuba: Editorial Pueblo y Educación; 2003.

24. González Rey, Fernando. Values and Their Significance in the Development of the Person. Rev. Temas. No 15; 1998.

25. United Bible Societies. God Speaks Today: The Bible with Deuterocanonical Books. Popular Version. Second Edition. Mexico City: United Bible Societies; 1987.

26. Lao Tse. Tao Teh Ching. In: Lin Yutang. Chinese Wisdom. Buenos Aires, Argentina: Colección ACADEMUS. Biblioteca Nueva; 1945.

27. Confucius in: Lin Yutang. The Wisdom of Confucius. Buenos Aires, Argentina: Ediciones Siglo Veinte; 1952.

28. Vishnu Sarma. Panchatantra. Third Edition. Havana, Cuba: Editorial Arte y Literatura; 2014.

29. Epictetus. Maxims, Exhortations, and Counsels. Barcelona, Spain: Biblioteca Orientalista. Editorial Teosófica; 1922.

30. Martí, José. Complete Works. Havana, Cuba: Editorial de Ciencias Sociales; 1991.

31. Solís, José Antonio. Sayings, Proverbs, Phrases, and Sentences. The Entire Treasure of Popular Wisdom from the People of Spain at Your Fingertips. Spain: El Arca de Papel Editores; 2003.

32. Sintes Pros, Jorge. Dictionary of Aphorisms, Proverbs, and Sayings. Barcelona, Spain: Editorial Sintes; 1954.

33. Cannobbio, Agustín. Chilean Sayings. Santiago de Chile: Encuadernación Barcelona; 1901.

34. Flores-Huerta, Samuel. Sayings or Proverbs. Thematic Compendium. Mexico: CopIt-arXives; 2016.

35. Álvarez de los Ríos, Tomás. The Book of Sayings. Camagüey, Cuba: Editorial Ácana; 2017.

36. Feijóo, Samuel. From Compliment to Banter, Oral Folklore of Cuba. Havana, Cuba: Editorial Letras Cubanas; 1981.

37. Feijóo, Samuel. *The Knowledge and Song of Juan Without Anything. Havana, Cuba: Editorial Letras Cubanas; 1984.*

38. Feijóo, Samuel. *The Knowledge of Juan Without Anything. Signs in the Expression of the People. Saying. Santa Clara, Cuba: Revista Signos. No 14. Year 5, No 2; January-April 1974.*

39. Valdés Jane, Ernesto. *Divinatory Sayings of the Shell and the Odun of Ifá. -In Cuban Santería- Documents for the History and Culture of Osha-Ifa in Cuba. First Edition: Proyecto Orunmila; 2007.*

40. Solís, José Antonio. *Sayings, Proverbs, Phrases, and Sentences. The Entire Treasure of Popular Wisdom from the People of Spain at Your Fingertips. Spain: El Arca de Papel Editores; 2003. p.41.*

41. Solís, José Antonio. *Sayings, Proverbs, Phrases, and Sentences. The Entire Treasure of Popular Wisdom from the People of Spain at Your Fingertips. Spain: El Arca de Papel Editores; 2003. p.106.*

42. Solís, José Antonio. *Sayings, Proverbs, Phrases, and Sentences. The Entire Treasure of Popular Wisdom from the People of Spain at Your Fingertips. Spain: El Arca de Papel Editores; 2003. p.30.*

43. Valdés Jane, Ernesto. *Divinatory Sayings of the Shell and the Odun of Ifá. -In Cuban Santería- Documents for the History and Culture of Osha-Ifa in Cuba. Sayings of (7-2) Odí tonti Eyioko. First Edition: Proyecto Orunmila; 2007. p.25.*

44. Solís, José Antonio. *Sayings, Proverbs, Phrases, and Sentences. The Entire Treasure of Popular Wisdom from the People of Spain at Your Fingertips. Spain: El Arca de Papel Editores; 2003. p.71.*

45. Sintes Pros, Jorge. *Dictionary of Aphorisms, Proverbs, and Sayings. Barcelona, Spain: Editorial Sintes; 1954. p.115.*

46. Feijóo, Samuel. The Knowledge of Juan Without Anything. Signs in the Expression of the People. Saying. Santa Clara, Cuba: Revista Signos. No 14. Year 5, No 2; January-April 1974. p.63.

47. Feijóo, Samuel. The Knowledge of Juan Without Anything. Signs in the Expression of the People. Saying. Santa Clara, Cuba: Revista Signos. No 14. Year 5, No 2; January-April 1974. p.52.

48. Sintes Pros, Jorge. Dictionary of Aphorisms, Proverbs, and Sayings. Barcelona, Spain: Editorial Sintes; 1954. p.169.

49. Feijóo, Samuel. The Knowledge of Juan Without Anything. Signs in the Expression of the People. Saying. Santa Clara, Cuba: Revista Signos. No 14. Year 5, No 2; January-April 1974. p.69.

50. Solís, José Antonio. Sayings, Proverbs, Phrases, and Sentences. The Entire Treasure of Popular Wisdom from the People of Spain at Your Fingertips. Spain: El Arca de Papel Editores; 2003. p.95.

51. United Bible Societies. God Speaks Today: The Bible with Deuterocanonical Books. Popular Version. Second Edition. Deuterocanonical Books. Sirach. Mexico City: United Bible Societies; 1987. p.109.

52. Cannobbio, Agustín. Chilean Sayings. Santiago de Chile: Encuadernación Barcelona; 1901. p.96.

53. Solís, José Antonio. Sayings, Proverbs, Phrases, and Sentences. The Entire Treasure of Popular Wisdom from the People of Spain at Your Fingertips. Spain: El Arca de Papel Editores; 2003. p.11.

54. Solís, José Antonio. Sayings, Proverbs, Phrases, and Sentences. The Entire Treasure of Popular Wisdom from the People of Spain at Your Fingertips. Spain: El Arca de Papel Editores; 2003. p.18.

55. Solís, José Antonio. Sayings, Proverbs, Phrases, and Sentences. The Entire Treasure of Popular Wisdom from the People of Spain at Your Fingertips. Spain: El Arca de Papel Editores; 2003. p.93.

56. Feijóo, Samuel. From Compliment to Banter, Oral Folklore of Cuba. Havana, Cuba: Editorial Letras Cubanas; 1981. p.39.

57. Feijóo, Samuel. The Knowledge of Juan Without Anything. Signs in the Expression of the People. Saying. Santa Clara, Cuba: Revista Signos. No 14. Year 5, No 2; January-April 1974. p.201.

58. Álvarez de los Ríos, Tomás. The Book of Sayings. Camagüey, Cuba: Editorial Ácana; 2017. p.16.

59. Feijóo, Samuel. The Knowledge and Song of Juan Without Anything. Havana, Cuba: Editorial Letras Cubanas; 1984. p.197.

60. United Bible Societies. God Speaks Today: The Bible with Deuterocanonical Books. Popular Version. Second Edition. Old Testament. Ecclesiastes. Mexico City: United Bible Societies; 1987. p.612.

61. Feijóo, Samuel. The Knowledge of Juan Without Anything. Signs in the Expression of the People. Saying. Santa Clara, Cuba: Revista Signos. No 14. Year 5, No 2; January-April 1974. p.54.

62. Feijóo, Samuel. The Knowledge of Juan Without Anything. Signs in the Expression of the People. Saying. Santa Clara, Cuba: Revista Signos. No 14. Year 5, No 2; January-April 1974. p.51.

63. The saying collected by Samuel Feijóo is: "Love and hate exaggerate." In: Feijóo, Samuel. The Knowledge of Juan Without Anything. Signs in the Expression of the People. Saying. Santa Clara, Cuba: Revista Signos. No 14. Year 5, No 2; January-April 1974. p.182.

64. Solís, José Antonio. Sayings, Proverbs, Phrases, and Sentences. The Entire Treasure of Popular Wisdom from the People of Spain at Your Fingertips. Spain: El Arca de Papel Editores; 2003. p.52.

65. Confucius in: Lin Yutang. Chinese Wisdom. Buenos Aires, Argentina: Colección ACADEMUS. Biblioteca Nueva; 1945. p.327.

66. Confucius in: Lin Yutang. Chinese Wisdom. Buenos Aires, Argentina: Colección ACADEMUS. Biblioteca Nueva; 1945. p.310.

67. Feijóo, Samuel. The Knowledge of Juan Without Anything. Signs in the Expression of the People. Saying. Santa Clara, Cuba: Revista Signos. No 14. Year 5, No 2; January-April 1974. p.54.

68. Confucius in: Lin Yutang. The Wisdom of Confucius. Buenos Aires, Argentina: Ediciones Siglo Veinte; 1952. p. 142.

69. Valdés Jane, Ernesto. Divinatory Sayings of the Shell and the Odun of Ifá. -In Cuban Santería- Documents for the History and Culture of Osha-Ifa in Cuba. Sayings of Ogunda Leni. First Edition: Proyecto Orunmila; 2007. p. 101.

70. Feijóo, Samuel. The Knowledge of Juan Without Anything. Signs in the Expression of the People. Saying. Santa Clara, Cuba: Revista Signos. No 14. Year 5, No 2; January-April 1974. p. 94.

71. Feijóo, Samuel. From Compliment to Banter, Oral Folklore of Cuba. Havana, Cuba: Editorial Letras Cubanas; 1981. p. 39.

72. Solís, José Antonio. Sayings, Proverbs, Phrases, and Sentences. The Entire Treasure of Popular Wisdom from the People of Spain at Your Fingertips. Spain: El Arca de Papel Editores; 2003. p. 132.

73. Valdés Jane, Ernesto. Divinatory Sayings of the Shell and the Odun of Ifá. -In Cuban Santería- Documents for the

History and Culture of Osha-Ifa in Cuba. Sayings of (8-6) Eyeúnle tonti Obara. First Edition: Proyecto Orunmila; 2007. p. 31.

74. Feijóo, Samuel. The Knowledge of Juan Without Anything. Signs in the Expression of the People. Saying. Santa Clara, Cuba: Revista Signos. No 14. Year 5, No 2; January-April 1974. p. 14.

75. Feijóo, Samuel. The Knowledge of Juan Without Anything. Signs in the Expression of the People. Saying. Santa Clara, Cuba: Revista Signos. No 14. Year 5, No 2; January-April 1974. p. 81.

76. Feijóo, Samuel. The Knowledge of Juan Without Anything. Signs in the Expression of the People. Saying. Santa Clara, Cuba: Revista Signos. No 14. Year 5, No 2; January-April 1974. p. 208.

77. Vishnu Sarma. Panchatantra. Third Edition. Havana, Cuba: Editorial Arte y Literatura; 2014. p. 166.

78. Feijóo, Samuel. The Knowledge of Juan Without Anything. Signs in the Expression of the People. Saying. Santa Clara, Cuba: Revista Signos. No 14. Year 5, No 2; January-April 1974. p. 78 and 86.

79. Feijóo, Samuel. The Knowledge of Juan Without Anything. Signs in the Expression of the People. Saying. Santa Clara, Cuba: Revista Signos. No 14. Year 5, No 2; January-April 1974. p. 57.

80. Flores-Huerta, Samuel. Sayings or Proverbs. Thematic Compendium. Mexico: CopIt-arXives; 2016. p. 94.

81. Feijóo, Samuel. The Knowledge of Juan Without Anything. Signs in the Expression of the People. Saying. Santa Clara, Cuba: Revista Signos. No 14. Year 5, No 2; January-April 1974. p. 159.

82. Feijóo, Samuel. The Knowledge of Juan Without Anything. Signs in the Expression of the People. Saying. Santa Clara,

Cuba: Revista Signos. No 14. Year 5, No 2; January-April 1974. p. 148.

83. Solís, José Antonio. Sayings, Proverbs, Phrases, and Sentences. The Entire Treasure of Popular Wisdom from the People of Spain at Your Fingertips. Spain: El Arca de Papel Editores; 2003. p. 54.

84. Solís, José Antonio. Sayings, Proverbs, Phrases, and Sentences. The Entire Treasure of Popular Wisdom from the People of Spain at Your Fingertips. Spain: El Arca de Papel Editores; 2003. p. 31.

85. Feijóo, Samuel. The Knowledge of Juan Without Anything. Signs in the Expression of the People. Saying. Santa Clara, Cuba: Revista Signos. No 14. Year 5, No 2; January-April 1974. p. 34.

86. Solís, José Antonio. Sayings, Proverbs, Phrases, and Sentences. The Entire Treasure of Popular Wisdom from the People of Spain at Your Fingertips. Spain: El Arca de Papel Editores; 2003. p. 38.

87. The saying collected by Ernesto Valdés Janes is: "The secret between two is not a secret." In: Valdés Jane, Ernesto. Divinatory Sayings of the Shell and the Odun of Ifá. -In Cuban Santería- Documents for the History and Culture of Osha-Ifa in Cuba. Sayings of (7-7) Odí tonti Odí. First Edition: Proyecto Orunmila; 2007. p. 27.

88. Solís, José Antonio. Sayings, Proverbs, Phrases, and Sentences. The Entire Treasure of Popular Wisdom from the People of Spain at Your Fingertips. Spain: El Arca de Papel Editores; 2003. p. 141.

89. Valdés Jane, Ernesto. Divinatory Sayings of the Shell and the Odun of Ifá. -In Cuban Santería- Documents for the History and Culture of Osha-Ifa in Cuba. Sayings of (13-2) Metanlá tonti Eyioko. First Edition: Proyecto Orunmila; 2007. p. 54.

90. Confucius in: Lin Yutang. The Wisdom of Confucius. Buenos Aires, Argentina: Ediciones Siglo Veinte; 1952. p. 121.

91. Feijóo, Samuel. The Knowledge of Juan Without Anything. Signs in the Expression of the People. Saying. Santa Clara, Cuba: Revista Signos. No 14. Year 5, No 2; January-April 1974. p. 83.

92. Solís, José Antonio. Sayings, Proverbs, Phrases, and Sentences. The Entire Treasure of Popular Wisdom. Spain: El Arca de Papel Editores; 2003. p. 75.

93. Solís, José Antonio. Sayings, Proverbs, Phrases, and Sentences. The Entire Treasure of Popular Wisdom. Spain: El Arca de Papel Editores; 2003. p.37.

94. Solís, José Antonio. Sayings, Proverbs, Phrases, and Sentences. The Entire Treasure of Popular Wisdom from the People of Spain at Your Fingertips. Spain: El Arca de Papel Editores; 2003. p.142.

95. Solís, José Antonio. Sayings, Proverbs, Phrases, and Sentences. The Entire Treasure of Popular Wisdom. Spain: El Arca de Papel Editores; 2003. p.53.

96. Valdés Jane, Ernesto. Divinatory Sayings of the Shell and the Odun of Ifá. -In Cuban Santería- Documents for the History and Culture of Osha-Ifa in Cuba. Sayings of (12-6) Eyilá tonti Obar. First Edition: Proyecto Orunmila; 2007. p. 50.

97. Feijóo, Samuel. The Knowledge of Juan Without Anything. Signs in the Expression of the People. Saying. Santa Clara, Cuba: Revista Signos. No 14. Year 5, No 2; January-April 1974. p.52.

98. United Bible Societies. God Speaks Today: The Bible with Deuterocanonical Books. Popular Version. Second Edition. Deuterocanonical Books. Sirach. Mexico City: United Bible Societies; 1987. p.124.

99. The saying collected by Samuel Feijóo is: "Do not prepare the spear when you have the antelope in front of you." In: Feijóo, Samuel. The Knowledge of Juan Without Anything. Signs in the Expression of the People. Saying. Santa Clara, Cuba: Revista Signos. No 14. Year 5, No 2; January-April 1974. p.210.

100. Martí, José. From Patria, New York. March 14, 1892. Our Ideas. In: Complete Works, Vol. I. Havana, Cuba: Editorial de Ciencias Sociales; 1991. p.316.

101. Feijóo, Samuel. The Knowledge of Juan Without Anything. Signs in the Expression of the People. Saying. Santa Clara, Cuba: Revista Signos. No 14. Year 5, No 2; January-April 1974. p.200.

102. Feijóo, Samuel. The Knowledge of Juan Without Anything. Signs in the Expression of the People. Saying. Santa Clara, Cuba: Revista Signos. No 14. Year 5, No 2; January-April 1974. p.87.

103. Feijóo, Samuel. The Knowledge of Juan Without Anything. Signs in the Expression of the People. Saying. Santa Clara, Cuba: Revista Signos. No 14. Year 5, No 2; January-April 1974. p.203.

104. Valdés Jane, Ernesto. Divinatory Sayings of the Shell and the Odun of Ifá. -In Cuban Santería- Documents for the History and Culture of Osha-Ifa in Cuba. Sayings of (12-2) Eyilá tonti Eyioko and of Irete Yekun. First Edition: Proyecto Orunmila; 2007. p.49 and 117.

105. Feijóo, Samuel. The Knowledge of Juan Without Anything. Signs in the Expression of the People. Saying. Santa Clara, Cuba: Revista Signos. No 14. Year 5, No 2; January-April 1974. p.158.

106. Feijóo, Samuel. The Knowledge of Juan Without Anything. Signs in the Expression of the People. Saying. Santa

Clara, Cuba: Revista Signos. No 14. Year 5, No 2; January-April 1974. p.83.

107. Feijóo, Samuel. From Compliment to Banter, Oral Folklore of Cuba. Havana, Cuba: Editorial Letras Cubanas; 1981. p.32.

108. Feijóo, Samuel. The Knowledge of Juan Without Anything. Signs in the Expression of the People. Saying. Santa Clara, Cuba: Revista Signos. No 14. Year 5, No 2; January-April 1974. p.88.

109. The saying collected by Samuel Feijóo is: "When one is about to fall, one does not see the hole." In: Feijóo, Samuel. The Knowledge of Juan Without Anything. Signs in the Expression of the People. Saying. Santa Clara, Cuba: Revista Signos. No 14. Year 5, No 2; January-April 1974. p.112.

110. Valdés Jane, Ernesto. Divinatory Sayings of the Shell and the Odun of Ifá. -In Cuban Santería- Documents for the History and Culture of Osha-Ifa in Cuba. Sayings of (4-10) Iroso tonti Ofún. First Edition: Proyecto Orunmila; 2007. p.15.

111. Feijóo, Samuel. From Compliment to Banter, Oral Folklore of Cuba. Havana, Cuba: Editorial Letras Cubanas; 1981. p.33.

112. Feijóo, Samuel. The Knowledge of Juan Without Anything. Signs in the Expression of the People. Saying. Santa Clara, Cuba: Revista Signos. No 14. Year 5, No 2; January-April 1974. p.203.

113. Valdés Jane, Ernesto. Divinatory Sayings of the Shell and the Odun of Ifá. -In Cuban Santería- Documents for the History and Culture of Osha-Ifa in Cuba. Sayings of (4-6) Iroso tonti Obara. First Edition: Proyecto Orunmila; 2007. p.14.

114. Feijóo, Samuel. From Compliment to Banter, Oral Folklore of Cuba. Havana, Cuba: Editorial Letras Cubanas; 1981. p.46.

115. United Bible Societies. God Speaks Today: The Bible with Deuterocanonical Books. Old Testament. Ecclesiastes. Popular Version. Second Edition. Mexico City: United Bible Societies; 1987. p.616.

116. Feijóo, Samuel. The Knowledge of Juan Without Anything. Signs in the Expression of the People. Saying. Santa Clara, Cuba: Revista Signos. No 14. Year 5, No 2; January-April 1974. p.163.

117. Confucius in: Lin Yutang. Chinese Wisdom. Buenos Aires, Argentina: Colección ACADEMUS. Biblioteca Nueva; 1945. p.291.

118. Solís, José Antonio. Sayings, Proverbs, Phrases, and Sentences. The Entire Treasure of Popular Wisdom from the People of Spain at Your Fingertips. Spain: El Arca de Papel Editores; 2003. p.127.

119. Valdés Jane, Ernesto. Divinatory Sayings of the Shell and the Odun of Ifá. -In Cuban Santería- Documents for the History and Culture of Osha-Ifa in Cuba. Sayings of (5-8) Oshé tonti Eyeúnle. First Edition: Proyecto Orunmila; 2007. p.19.

120. Solís, José Antonio. Sayings, Proverbs, Phrases, and Sentences. The Entire Treasure of Popular Wisdom from the People of Spain at Your Fingertips. Spain: El Arca de Papel Editores; 2003. p.33.

121. Flores-Huerta, Samuel. Sayings or Proverbs. Thematic Compendium. Mexico: CopIt-arXives; 2016. p.75.

122. Sintes Pros, Jorge. Dictionary of Aphorisms, Proverbs, and Sayings. Barcelona, Spain: Editorial Sintes; 1954. p.45.

123. Feijóo, Samuel. The Knowledge of Juan Without Anything. Signs in the Expression of the People. Saying. Santa Clara, Cuba: Revista Signos. No 14. Year 5, No 2; January-April 1974. p.105.

124. Solís, José Antonio. Sayings, Proverbs, Phrases, and Sentences. The Entire Treasure of Popular Wisdom from the People of Spain at Your Fingertips. Spain: El Arca de Papel Editores; 2003. p.77.

125. Feijóo, Samuel. The Knowledge of Juan Without Anything. Signs in the Expression of the People. Saying. Santa Clara, Cuba: Revista Signos. No 14. Year 5, No 2; January-April 1974. p.32.

126. Solís, José Antonio. Sayings, Proverbs, Phrases, and Sentences. The Entire Treasure of Popular Wisdom from the People of Spain at Your Fingertips. Spain: El Arca de Papel Editores; 2003. p.61.

127. Cannobbio, Agustín. Chilean Sayings. Santiago de Chile: Encuadernación Barcelona; 1901. p.36.

128. The saying collected by Ernesto Valdés Jane was: "Man carries two sacks: one to win and one to lose." In: Valdés Jane, Ernesto. Divinatory Sayings of the Shell and the Odun of Ifá. - In Cuban Santería- Documents for the History and Culture of Osha-Ifa in Cuba. Sayings of Ogunda Leni. First Edition: Proyecto Orunmila; 2007. p.101.

129. Solís, José Antonio. Sayings, Proverbs, Phrases, and Sentences. The Entire Treasure of Popular Wisdom from the People of Spain at Your Fingertips. Spain: El Arca de Papel Editores; 2003. p.79.

130. Solís, José Antonio. Sayings, Proverbs, Phrases, and Sentences. The Entire Treasure of Popular Wisdom from the People of Spain at Your Fingertips. Spain: El Arca de Papel Editores; 2003. p.79.

131. Feijóo, Samuel. The Knowledge of Juan Without Anything. Signs in the Expression of the People. Saying. Santa Clara, Cuba: Revista Signos. No 14. Year 5, No 2; January-April 1974. p.210.

132. Solís, José Antonio. Sayings, Proverbs, Phrases, and Sentences. The Entire Treasure of Popular Wisdom from the People of Spain at Your Fingertips. Spain: El Arca de Papel Editores; 2003. p.59.

133. Solís, José Antonio. Sayings, Proverbs, Phrases, and Sentences. The Entire Treasure of Popular Wisdom from the People of Spain at Your Fingertips. Spain: El Arca de Papel Editores; 2003. p.140.

134. Solís, José Antonio. Sayings, Proverbs, Phrases, and Sentences. The Entire Treasure of Popular Wisdom from the People of Spain at Your Fingertips. Spain: El Arca de Papel Editores; 2003. p.21.

135. Feijóo, Samuel. The Knowledge of Juan Without Anything. Signs in the Expression of the People. Saying. Santa Clara, Cuba: Revista Signos. No 14. Year 5, No 2; January-April 1974. p.199.

136. Solís, José Antonio. Sayings, Proverbs, Phrases, and Sentences. The Entire Treasure of Popular Wisdom. Spain: El Arca de Papel Editores; 2003. p.35.

137. Solís, José Antonio. Sayings, Proverbs, Phrases, and Sentences. The Entire Treasure of Popular Wisdom. Spain: El Arca de Papel Editores; 2003. p.68.

138. Sintes Pros, Jorge. Dictionary of Aphorisms, Proverbs, and Sayings. Barcelona, Spain: Editorial Sintes; 1954. p.292.

139. Cannobbio, Agustín. Chilean Sayings. Santiago de Chile: Encuadernación Barcelona; 1901. p.25.

140. Feijóo, Samuel. From Compliment to Banter, Oral Folklore of Cuba. Havana, Cuba: Editorial Letras Cubanas; 1981. p.30.

141. Confucius in: Lin Yutang. The Wisdom of Confucius. Buenos Aires, Argentina: Ediciones Siglo Veinte; 1952. p.174.

142. Sintes Pros, Jorge. Dictionary of Aphorisms, Proverbs, and Sayings. Barcelona, Spain: Editorial Sintes; 1954. p.268.

143. The saying collected by Samuel Feijóo is: "The lame person outpaces the one who is off the path." In: Feijóo, Samuel. The Knowledge of Juan Without Anything. Signs in the Expression of the People. Saying. Santa Clara, Cuba: Revista Signos. No 14. Year 5, No 2; January-April 1974. p.114.

144. Feijóo, Samuel. From Compliment to Banter, Oral Folklore of Cuba. Havana, Cuba: Editorial Letras Cubanas; 1981. p.19.

145. Sintes Pros, Jorge. Dictionary of Aphorisms, Proverbs, and Sayings. Barcelona, Spain: Editorial Sintes; 1954. p.158, 256.

146. Solís, José Antonio. Sayings, Proverbs, Phrases, and Sentences. The Entire Treasure of Popular Wisdom from the People of Spain at Your Fingertips. Spain: El Arca de Papel Editores; 2003. p.118.

147. Martí, José. Complete Works. Vol. II. Commemorative Edition of the 50th Anniversary of His Death. Havana: Editorial Lex; 1946. p.1892.

148. Feijóo, Samuel. The Knowledge of Juan Without Anything. Signs in the Expression of the People. Saying. Santa Clara, Cuba: Revista Signos. No 14. Year 5, No 2; January-April 1974. p.54.

149. Feijóo, Samuel. The Knowledge of Juan Without Anything. Signs in the Expression of the People. Saying. Santa Clara, Cuba: Revista Signos. No 14. Year 5, No 2; January-April 1974. p.162.

150. Solís, José Antonio. Sayings, Proverbs, Phrases, and Sentences. The Entire Treasure of Popular Wisdom from the People of Spain at Your Fingertips. Spain: El Arca de Papel Editores; 2003. p.93.

151. Solís, José Antonio. Sayings, Proverbs, Phrases, and Sentences. The Entire Treasure of Popular Wisdom from the

People of Spain at Your Fingertips. Spain: El Arca de Papel Editores; 2003. p.93.

152. The saying collected by José Antonio Solís is: "Take your goods to the market, some will say it's good, and others will say it's bad." In: Solís, José Antonio. Sayings, Proverbs, Phrases, and Sentences. The Entire Treasure of Popular Wisdom from the People of Spain at Your Fingertips. Spain: El Arca de Papel Editores; 2003. p.140.

153. Álvarez de los Ríos, Tomás. The Book of Sayings. Camagüey, Cuba: Editorial Ácana; 2017. p.103.

154. Feijóo, Samuel. The Knowledge of Juan Without Anything. Signs in the Expression of the People. Saying. Santa Clara, Cuba: Revista Signos. No 14. Year 5, No 2; January-April 1974. p.110.

155. Feijóo, Samuel. The Knowledge of Juan Without Anything. Signs in the Expression of the People. Saying. Santa Clara, Cuba: Revista Signos. No 14. Year 5, No 2; January-April 1974. p.100.

156. Valdés Jane, Ernesto. Divinatory Sayings of the Shell and the Odun of Ifá. -In Cuban Santería- Documents for the History and Culture of Osha-Ifa in Cuba. Sayings of Odi Trupon. First Edition: Proyecto Orunmila; 2007. p.85.

157. Feijóo, Samuel. From Compliment to Banter, Oral Folklore of Cuba. Havana, Cuba: Editorial Letras Cubanas; 1981. p.46.

158. Feijóo, Samuel. The Knowledge of Juan Without Anything. Signs in the Expression of the People. Saying. Santa Clara, Cuba: Revista Signos. No 14. Year 5, No 2; January-April 1974. p.99.

159. Solís, José Antonio. Sayings, Proverbs, Phrases, and Sentences. The Entire Treasure of Popular Wisdom from the People of Spain at Your Fingertips. Spain: El Arca de Papel Editores; 2003. p.31.

160. Solís, José Antonio. Sayings, Proverbs, Phrases, and Sentences. The Entire Treasure of Popular Wisdom from the People of Spain at Your Fingertips. Spain: El Arca de Papel Editores; 2003. p.31.

161. Confucius in: Lin Yutang. The Wisdom of Confucius. Buenos Aires, Argentina: Ediciones Siglo Veinte; 1952. p.29.

162. Sintes Pros, Jorge. Dictionary of Aphorisms, Proverbs, and Sayings. Barcelona, Spain: Editorial Sintes; 1954. p.99.

163. Feijóo, Samuel. The Knowledge of Juan Without Anything. Signs in the Expression of the People. Saying. Santa Clara, Cuba: Revista Signos. No 14. Year 5, No 2; January-April 1974. p.208.

164. Feijóo, Samuel. The Knowledge of Juan Without Anything. Signs in the Expression of the People. Saying. Santa Clara, Cuba: Revista Signos. No 14. Year 5, No 2; January-April 1974. p.178.

165. Sintes Pros, Jorge. Dictionary of Aphorisms, Proverbs, and Sayings. Barcelona, Spain: Editorial Sintes; 1954. p.134.

166. Feijóo, Samuel. From Compliment to Banter, Oral Folklore of Cuba. Havana, Cuba: Editorial Letras Cubanas; 1981. p.26.

167. Valdés Jane, Ernesto. Divinatory Sayings of the Shell and the Odun of Ifá. -In Cuban Santería- Documents for the History and Culture of Osha-Ifa in Cuba. Sayings of (14-2) Merinlá Tonti Eyioko. First Edition: Proyecto Orunmila; 2007. p.57.

168. Feijóo, Samuel. The Knowledge of Juan Without Anything. Signs in the Expression of the People. Saying. Santa Clara, Cuba: Revista Signos. No 14. Year 5, No 2; January-April 1974. p.159.

169. Valdés Jane, Ernesto. Divinatory Sayings of the Shell and the Odun of Ifá. -In Cuban Santería- Documents for the History and Culture of Osha-Ifa in Cuba. Sayings of (14-2)

Merinlá Tonti Eyioko. First Edition: Proyecto Orunmila; 2007. p.57.

170. Valdés Jane, Ernesto. Divinatory Sayings of the Shell and the Odun of Ifá. -In Cuban Santería- Documents for the History and Culture of Osha-Ifa in Cuba. Sayings of (3-10) Ogundá tonti Ofún. First Edition: Proyecto Orunmila; 2007. p.11.

171. Feijóo, Samuel. The Knowledge of Juan Without Anything. Signs in the Expression of the People. Saying. Santa Clara, Cuba: Revista Signos. No 14. Year 5, No 2; January-April 1974. p.149.

172. Feijóo, Samuel. The Knowledge of Juan Without Anything. Signs in the Expression of the People. Saying. Santa Clara, Cuba: Revista Signos. No 14. Year 5, No 2; January-April 1974. p.105.

173. Cannobbio, Agustín. Chilean Sayings. Santiago de Chile: Encuadernación Barcelona; 1901. p.42.

174. Solís, José Antonio. Sayings, Proverbs, Phrases, and Sentences. The Entire Treasure of Popular Wisdom from the People of Spain at Your Fingertips. Spain: El Arca de Papel Editores; 2003. p.120.

175. Flores-Huerta, Samuel. Sayings or Proverbs. Thematic Compendium. Mexico: CopIt-arXives; 2016. p.65.

176. Flores-Huerta, Samuel. Sayings or Proverbs. Thematic Compendium. Mexico: CopIt-arXives; 2016. p.30.

177. The Quran. In: Pérez Betancourt, A. et al. Error Hunting. Havana, Cuba: Editorial Ciencias Sociales; 1990. p.54.

178. Feijóo, Samuel. From Compliment to Banter, Oral Folklore of Cuba. Havana, Cuba: Editorial Letras Cubanas; 1981. p.40.

179. Valdés Jane, Ernesto. Divinatory Sayings of the Shell and the Odun of Ifá. -In Cuban Santería- Documents for the History and Culture of Osha-Ifa in Cuba. Sayings of (4-15)

Iroso tonti Marunlá. First Edition: Proyecto Orunmila; 2007. p.16.

180. Valdés Jane, Ernesto. Divinatory Sayings of the Shell and the Odun of Ifá. -In Cuban Santería- Documents for the History and Culture of Osha-Ifa in Cuba. Sayings of (1-7) Okana tonti Odí. First Edition: Proyecto Orunmila; 2007. p.3.

181. Valdés Jane, Ernesto. Divinatory Sayings of the Shell and the Odun of Ifá. -In Cuban Santería- Documents for the History and Culture of Osha-Ifa in Cuba. Sayings of (4-12) Iroso tonti Eyilá. First Edition: Proyecto Orunmila; 2007. p.16.

182. Valdés Jane, Ernesto. Divinatory Sayings of the Shell and the Odun of Ifá. -In Cuban Santería- Documents for the History and Culture of Osha-Ifa in Cuba. Sayings of (6-12) Obara tonti Eyilá. First Edition: Proyecto Orunmila; 2007. p.24.

183. Solís, José Antonio. Sayings, Proverbs, Phrases, and Sentences. The Entire Treasure of Popular Wisdom from the People of Spain at Your Fingertips. Spain: El Arca de Papel Editores; 2003. p.72.

184. United Bible Societies. God Speaks Today: The Bible with Deuterocanonical Books. Popular Version. Second Edition. Old Testament. Proverbs. Mexico City: United Bible Societies; 1987. p.586.

185. Solís, José Antonio. Sayings, Proverbs, Phrases, and Sentences. The Entire Treasure of Popular Wisdom from the People of Spain at Your Fingertips. Spain: El Arca de Papel Editores; 2003. p.135.

186. Valdés Jane, Ernesto. Divinatory Sayings of the Shell and the Odun of Ifá. -In Cuban Santería- Documents for the History and Culture of Osha-Ifa in Cuba. Sayings of (6-3) Obara tonti Ogundá, (10-4) Ofún tonti Iroso, Ofún Koso, and

Ogunda Ka. First Edition: Proyecto Orunmila; 2007. pp.21, 41, 102, 125.

187. Cannobbio, Agustín. Chilean Sayings. Santiago de Chile: Encuadernación Barcelona; 1901. p.89.

188. Feijóo, Samuel. The Knowledge of Juan Without Anything. Signs in the Expression of the People. Saying. Santa Clara, Cuba: Revista Signos. No 14. Year 5, No 2; January-April 1974. p.158.

189. Valdés Jane, Ernesto. Divinatory Sayings of the Shell and the Odun of Ifá. -In Cuban Santería- Documents for the History and Culture of Osha-Ifa in Cuba. Sayings of (4-11) Iroso tonti Ojuani, (6-6) Obara tonti Obara, (10-7) Ofún tonti Odí, and Okana Fun. First Edition: Proyecto Orunmila; 2007. pp.15, 22, 42, 99.

190. Solís, José Antonio. Sayings, Proverbs, Phrases, and Sentences. The Entire Treasure of Popular Wisdom from the People of Spain at Your Fingertips. Spain: El Arca de Papel Editores; 2003. p.70.

191. Flores-Huerta, Samuel. Sayings or Proverbs. Thematic Compendium. Mexico: CopIt-arXives; 2016. p.41.

192. The saying collected by José Antonio Solís is: "The suitor who chases many, sleeps with none." In: Solís, José Antonio. Sayings, Proverbs, Phrases, and Sentences. The Entire Treasure of Popular Wisdom. Spain: El Arca de Papel Editores; 2003. p.53.

193. Feijóo, Samuel. The Knowledge of Juan Without Anything. Signs in the Expression of the People. Saying. Santa Clara, Cuba: Revista Signos. No 14. Year 5, No 2; January-April 1974. p.127.

194. Solís, José Antonio. Sayings, Proverbs, Phrases, and Sentences. The Entire Treasure of Popular Wisdom from the People of Spain at Your Fingertips. La Coruña, Spain: El Arca de Papel Editores; 2003. p.51.

195. Flores-Huerta, Samuel. Sayings or Proverbs. Thematic Compendium. Mexico: CopIt-arXives; 2016. p.55.

196. Solís, José Antonio. Sayings, Proverbs, Phrases, and Sentences. The Entire Treasure of Popular Wisdom from the People of Spain at Your Fingertips. La Coruña, Spain: El Arca de Papel Editores; 2003. p.113.

197. Solís, José Antonio. Sayings, Proverbs, Phrases, and Sentences. The Entire Treasure of Popular Wisdom from the People of Spain at Your Fingertips. La Coruña, Spain: El Arca de Papel Editores; 2003. p.67.

198. Solís, José Antonio. Sayings, Proverbs, Phrases, and Sentences. The Entire Treasure of Popular Wisdom from the People of Spain at Your Fingertips. La Coruña, Spain: El Arca de Papel Editores; 2003. p.26.

199. United Bible Societies. God Speaks Today: The Bible with Deuterocanonical Books. Popular Version. Second Edition. Deuterocanonical Books. Ecclesiasticus. Mexico City: United Bible Societies; 1987. p.105.

200. Solís, José Antonio. Sayings, Proverbs, Phrases, and Sentences. The Entire Treasure of Popular Wisdom from the People of Spain at Your Fingertips. La Coruña, Spain: El Arca de Papel Editores; 2003. p.130.

201. Martínez Furé, Rogelio. Anonymous African Poetry. Havana, Cuba: Instituto Cubano del Libro; 1968. p.133.

202. Feijóo, Samuel. From Compliment to Banter, Oral Folklore of Cuba. Havana, Cuba: Editorial Letras Cubanas; 1981. p.32.

203. Solís, José Antonio. Sayings, Proverbs, Phrases, and Sentences. The Entire Treasure of Popular Wisdom from the People of Spain at Your Fingertips. Spain: El Arca de Papel Editores; 2003. p.116.

204. Solís, José Antonio. Sayings, Proverbs, Phrases, and Sentences. The Entire Treasure of Popular Wisdom from the

People of Spain at Your Fingertips. Spain: El Arca de Papel Editores; 2003. p.116.

205. Vishnu Sarma. Panchatantra. Third Edition. Havana, Cuba: Editorial Arte y Literatura; 2014. pp.284, 288.

206. United Bible Societies. God Speaks Today: The Bible with Deuterocanonical Books. Popular Version. Second Edition. Old Testament. Proverbs. Mexico City: United Bible Societies; 1987. p.592.

207. United Bible Societies. God Speaks Today: The Bible with Deuterocanonical Books. Popular Version. Second Edition. Old Testament. Proverbs. Mexico City: United Bible Societies; 1987. pp.590, 593.

208. Feijóo, Samuel. The Knowledge of Juan Without Anything. Signs in the Expression of the People. Saying. Santa Clara, Cuba: Revista Signos. No 14. Year 5, No 2; January-April 1974. p.31.

209. Valdés Jane, Ernesto. Divinatory Sayings of the Shell and the Odun of Ifá. -In Cuban Santería- Documents for the History and Culture of Osha-Ifa in Cuba. Sayings of (10-16) Ofún tonti Merindilogún. First Edition: Proyecto Orunmila; 2007. p.45.

210. Solís, José Antonio. Sayings, Proverbs, Phrases, and Sentences. The Entire Treasure of Popular Wisdom from the People of Spain at Your Fingertips. Spain: El Arca de Papel Editores; 2003. p.127.

211. Feijóo, Samuel. The Knowledge of Juan Without Anything. Signs in the Expression of the People. Saying. Santa Clara, Cuba: Revista Signos. No 14. Year 5, No 2; January-April 1974. p.206.

212. United Bible Societies. God Speaks Today: The Bible with Deuterocanonical Books. Popular Version. Second Edition. Old Testament. Ecclesiastes. Mexico City: United Bible Societies; 1987. p.617.

213. Valdés Jane, Ernesto. Divinatory Sayings of the Shell and the Odun of Ifá. -In Cuban Santería- Documents for the History and Culture of Osha-Ifa in Cuba. Sayings of Oyekun Funda and (2-3) Eyioko tonti Ogundá. First Edition: Proyecto Orunmila; 2007. pp.5, 77.

214. Valdés Jane, Ernesto. Divinatory Sayings of the Shell and the Odun of Ifá. -In Cuban Santería- Documents for the History and Culture of Osha-Ifa in Cuba. Sayings of (2-4) Eyioko tonti Iroso. First Edition: Proyecto Orunmila; 2007. p.6.

215. Valdés Jane, Ernesto. Divinatory Sayings of the Shell and the Odun of Ifá. -In Cuban Santería- Documents for the History and Culture of Osha-Ifa in Cuba. Sayings of (2-4) Eyioko tonti Iroso. First Edition: Proyecto Orunmila; 2007. p.5.

216. Valdés Jane, Ernesto. Divinatory Sayings of the Shell and the Odun of Ifá. -In Cuban Santería- Documents for the History and Culture of Osha-Ifa in Cuba. Sayings of (7-4) Odí tonti Iroso. First Edition: Proyecto Orunmila; 2007. p.26.

217. The sayings collected by Jorge Sintes Pros are: "There is no one more blind than the one who does not want to see" and "There is no one more deaf than the one who does not want to hear." In: Sintes Pros, Jorge. Dictionary of Aphorisms, Proverbs, and Sayings. Barcelona, Spain: Editorial Sintes; 1954. pp.75, 258.

218. Solís, José Antonio. Sayings, Proverbs, Phrases, and Sentences. The Entire Treasure of Popular Wisdom from the People of Spain at Your Fingertips. Spain: El Arca de Papel Editores; 2003. p.123.

219. Feijóo, Samuel. The Knowledge of Juan Without Anything. Signs in the Expression of the People. Saying. Santa Clara, Cuba: Revista Signos. No 14. Year 5, No 2; January-April 1974. p.158.

220. Feijóo, Samuel. The Knowledge of Juan Without Anything. Signs in the Expression of the People. Saying. Santa Clara, Cuba: Revista Signos. No 14. Year 5, No 2; January-April 1974. p.114.

221. Cannobbio, Agustín. Chilean Sayings. Santiago, Chile: Encuadernación Barcelona; 1901. p.108.

222. Valdés Jane, Ernesto. Divinatory Sayings of the Shell and the Odun of Ifá. -In Cuban Santería- Documents for the History and Culture of Osha-Ifa in Cuba. Sayings of (4-4) Iroso tonti Iroso. First Edition: Proyecto Orunmila; 2007. p.14.

223. Valdés Jane, Ernesto. Divinatory Sayings of the Shell and the Odun of Ifá. -In Cuban Santería- Documents for the History and Culture of Osha-Ifa in Cuba. Sayings of (6-15) Obara tonti Marunlá. First Edition: Proyecto Orunmila; 2007. p.24.

224. Valdés Jane, Ernesto. Divinatory Sayings of the Shell and the Odun of Ifá. -In Cuban Santería- Documents for the History and Culture of Osha-Ifa in Cuba. Sayings of (7-14) Odí tonti Merinlá. First Edition: Proyecto Orunmila; 2007. pp.26, 29.

225. Valdés Jane, Ernesto. Divinatory Sayings of the Shell and the Odun of Ifá. -In Cuban Santería- Documents for the History and Culture of Osha-Ifa in Cuba. Sayings of (16-4) Merindilogún tonti Iroso. First Edition: Proyecto Orunmila; 2007. p.64.

226. Valdés Jane, Ernesto. Divinatory Sayings of the Shell and the Odun of Ifá. -In Cuban Santería- Documents for the History and Culture of Osha-Ifa in Cuba. Sayings of (16-4) Merindilogún tonti Iroso. First Edition: Proyecto Orunmila; 2007. p.64.

227. Álvarez de los Ríos, Tomás. The Book of Sayings. Camagüey, Cuba: Editorial Ácana; 2017. p.53.

228. Valdés Jane, Ernesto. Divinatory Sayings of the Shell and the Odun of Ifá. -In Cuban Santería- Documents for the History and Culture of Osha-Ifa in Cuba. Sayings of (12-9) Eyilá tonti Osá. First Edition: Proyecto Orunmila; 2007. p.51.

229. Feijóo, Samuel. The Knowledge of Juan Without Anything. Signs in the Expression of the People. Saying. Santa Clara, Cuba: Revista Signos. No 14. Year 5, No 2; January-April 1974. p.186.

230. Solís, José Antonio. Sayings, Proverbs, Phrases, and Sentences. The Entire Treasure of Popular Wisdom from the People of Spain at Your Fingertips. Spain: El Arca de Papel Editores; 2003. p.38.

231. Flores-Huerta, Samuel. Sayings or Proverbs. Thematic Compendium. Mexico: CopIt-arXives; 2016. p.57.

232. The saying collected by José Antonio Solís is: "Bad advice will be given to me by someone who has none for himself." In: Solís, José Antonio. Sayings, Proverbs, Phrases, and Sentences. The Entire Treasure of Popular Wisdom. Spain: El Arca de Papel Editores; 2003. p.96.

233. United Bible Societies. God Speaks Today: The Bible with Deuterocanonical Books. Popular Version. Second Edition. Deuterocanonical Books. Ecclesiasticus. Mexico City: United Bible Societies; 1987. p.97.

234. Feijóo, Samuel. The Knowledge of Juan Without Anything. Signs in the Expression of the People. Saying. Santa Clara, Cuba: Revista Signos. No 14. Year 5, No 2; January-April 1974. p.162.

235. Feijóo, Samuel. The Knowledge of Juan Without Anything. Signs in the Expression of the People. Saying. Santa Clara, Cuba: Revista Signos. No 14. Year 5, No 2; January-April 1974. p.130.

236. Feijóo, Samuel. The Knowledge of Juan Without Anything. Signs in the Expression of the People. Saying. Santa

Clara, Cuba: Revista Signos. No 14. Year 5, No 2; January-April 1974. p.191.

237. Valdés Jane, Ernesto. Divinatory Sayings of the Shell and the Odun of Ifá. -In Cuban Santería- Documents for the History and Culture of Osha-Ifa in Cuba. Sayings of (10-14) Ofún tonti Merinlá. First Edition: Proyecto Orunmila; 2007. pp.44, 124.

238. Valdés Jane, Ernesto. Divinatory Sayings of the Shell and the Odun of Ifá. -In Cuban Santería- Documents for the History and Culture of Osha-Ifa in Cuba. Sayings of (9-7) Osá tonti Odí. First Edition: Proyecto Orunmila; 2007. p.37.

239. Sintes Pros, Jorge. Dictionary of Aphorisms, Proverbs, and Sayings. Barcelona, Spain: Editorial Sintes; 1954. p.179.

240. Álvarez de los Ríos, Tomás. The Book of Sayings. Camagüey, Cuba: Editorial Ácana; 2017. p.25.

241. United Bible Societies. God Speaks Today: The Bible with Deuterocanonical Books. Popular Version. Second Edition. Old Testament. Proverbs. Mexico City: United Bible Societies; 1987. p.595.

242. Flores-Huerta, Samuel. Sayings or Proverbs. Thematic Compendium. Mexico: CopIt-arXives; 2016. p.50.

243. Flores-Huerta, Samuel. Sayings or Proverbs. Thematic Compendium. Mexico: CopIt-arXives; 2016. p.50.

244. Flores-Huerta, Samuel. Sayings or Proverbs. Thematic Compendium. Mexico: CopIt-arXives; 2016. p.51.

245. Sintes Pros, Jorge. Dictionary of Aphorisms, Proverbs, and Sayings. Barcelona, Spain: Editorial Sintes; 1954. p.231.

246. Feijóo, Samuel. The Knowledge of Juan Without Anything. Signs in the Expression of the People. Saying. Santa Clara, Cuba: Revista Signos. No 14. Year 5, No 2; January-April 1974. p.59.

247. Solís, José Antonio. Sayings, Proverbs, Phrases, and Sentences. The Entire Treasure of Popular Wisdom from the

People of Spain at Your Fingertips. Spain: El Arca de Papel Editores; 2003. p.32.

248. Feijóo, Samuel. The Knowledge of Juan Without Anything. Signs in the Expression of the People. Saying. Santa Clara, Cuba: Revista Signos. No 14. Year 5, No 2; January-April 1974. p.163.

249. Feijóo, Samuel. The Knowledge of Juan Without Anything. Signs in the Expression of the People. Saying. Santa Clara, Cuba: Revista Signos. No 14. Year 5, No 2; January-April 1974. p.158.

250. Vishnu Sarma. Panchatantra. Third Edition. Havana, Cuba: Editorial Arte y Literatura; 2014. p.178.

251. Feijóo, Samuel. The Knowledge of Juan Without Anything. Signs in the Expression of the People. Saying. Santa Clara, Cuba: Revista Signos. No 14. Year 5, No 2; January-April 1974. p.15.

252. Feijóo, Samuel. The Knowledge of Juan Without Anything. Signs in the Expression of the People. Saying. Santa Clara, Cuba: Revista Signos. No 14. Year 5, No 2; January-April 1974. p.24.

253. Valdés Jane, Ernesto. Divinatory Sayings of the Shell and the Odun of Ifá. -In Cuban Santería- Documents for the History and Culture of Osha-Ifa in Cuba. Sayings of (5-15) Oshé tonti Marunlá. First Edition: Proyecto Orunmila; 2007. p.20.

254. Feijóo, Samuel. The Knowledge of Juan Without Anything. Signs in the Expression of the People. Saying. Santa Clara, Cuba: Revista Signos. No 14. Year 5, No 2; January-April 1974. p.52.

255. Feijóo, Samuel. The Knowledge of Juan Without Anything. Signs in the Expression of the People. Saying. Santa Clara, Cuba: Revista Signos. No 14. Year 5, No 2; January-April 1974. p.51.

256. Valdés Jane, Ernesto. Divinatory Sayings of the Shell and the Odun of Ifá. -In Cuban Santería- Documents for the History and Culture of Osha-Ifa in Cuba. Sayings of (8-5) Eyeúnle tonti Oshé and Ogbe She. First Edition: Proyecto Orunmila; 2007. pp.31, 74.

257. Valdés Jane, Ernesto. Divinatory Sayings of the Shell and the Odun of Ifá. -In Cuban Santería- Documents for the History and Culture of Osha-Ifa in Cuba. Sayings of (12-2) Eyilá tonti Eyioko and Otrupon Yekun. First Edition: Proyecto Orunmila; 2007. pp.49, 111.

258. Flores-Huerta, Samuel. Sayings or Proverbs. Thematic Compendium. Mexico: CopIt-arXives; 2016. p.30.

259. Valdés Jane, Ernesto. Divinatory Sayings of the Shell and the Odun of Ifá. -In Cuban Santería- Documents for the History and Culture of Osha-Ifa in Cuba. Sayings of (15-6) Marunlá tonti Obara. First Edition: Proyecto Orunmila; 2007. p.61.

260. Valdés Jane, Ernesto. Divinatory Sayings of the Shell and the Odun of Ifá. -In Cuban Santería- Documents for the History and Culture of Osha-Ifa in Cuba. Sayings of (4-15) Iroso tonti Marunlá. First Edition: Proyecto Orunmila; 2007. p.16.

261. Valdés Jane, Ernesto. Divinatory Sayings of the Shell and the Odun of Ifá. -In Cuban Santería- Documents for the History and Culture of Osha-Ifa in Cuba. Sayings of (4-15) Iroso tonti Marunlá. First Edition: Proyecto Orunmila; 2007. p.16.

262. The saying collected by José Antonio Solís is: "There is no worse blind man than the one who, being blind, believes he can see." In: Solís, José Antonio. Sayings, Proverbs, Phrases, and Sentences. The Entire Treasure of Popular Wisdom from the People of Spain at Your Fingertips. Spain: El Arca de Papel Editores; 2003. p.116.

263. *Flores-Huerta, Samuel.* Sayings or Proverbs. Thematic Compendium. *Mexico: CopIt-arXives; 2016. p.195.*

264. Feijóo, Samuel. The Knowledge of Juan Without Anything. Signs in the Expression of the People. Saying. Santa Clara, Cuba: Revista Signos. No 14. Year 5, No 2; January-April 1974. p.30.

265. Solís, José Antonio. Sayings, Proverbs, Phrases, and Sentences. The Entire Treasure of Popular Wisdom from the People of Spain at Your Fingertips. Spain: El Arca de Papel Editores; 2003. p.69.

266. Valdés Jane, Ernesto. Divinatory Sayings of the Shell and the Odun of Ifá. -In Cuban Santería- Documents for the History and Culture of Osha-Ifa in Cuba. Sayings of (2-8) Eyioko tonti Eyeúnle. First Edition: Proyecto Orunmila; 2007. p.6.

267. Solís, José Antonio. Sayings, Proverbs, Phrases, and Sentences. The Entire Treasure of Popular Wisdom from the People of Spain at Your Fingertips. Spain: El Arca de Papel Editores; 2003. p.29.

268. Sintes Pros, Jorge. Dictionary of Aphorisms, Proverbs, and Sayings. Barcelona, Spain: Editorial Sintes; 1954. p.183.

269. Solís, José Antonio. Sayings, Proverbs, Phrases, and Sentences. The Entire Treasure of Popular Wisdom from the People of Spain at Your Fingertips. Spain: El Arca de Papel Editores; 2003. p.115.

270- Álvarez de los Ríos Tomás. The Book of Proverbs. Camagüey, Cuba: Editorial Ácana, 2017, p. 79.

271- Sintes Pros Jorge. Dictionary of Aphorisms, Proverbs, and Sayings. Barcelona, Spain: Editorial Sintes, 1954, p. 119.

272- Hesiod. in: Epictetus. Maxims, Exhortations, and Counsel. Barcelona, Spain: Biblioteca Orientalista. Editorial Teosófica, 1922, p. 93.

273- Vishnu Sarma. Panchatantra. Editorial Arte y Literatura.

Third Edition. Havana, 'Cuba: 2014, p. 214.
274- Valdés Jane Ernesto. Proverbial Divination of the Caracol and the Odun of Ifá. -In Cuban Santería- Documents for the History and Culture of Osha-Ifa in Cuba. Proverbs from (3-1) Ogundá tonti Okana. First Edition: Proyecto Orunmila, 2007, p. 8.
275- United Bible Societies. God Speaks Today. The Bible with Deuterocanonicals. Old Testament. Proverbs. Popular Version. Second Edition. Mexico City, Mexico: United Bible Societies, 1987, p. 604.
276- United Bible Societies. God Speaks Today. The Bible with Deuterocanonicals. Old Testament. Proverbs. Popular Version. Second Edition. Mexico City, Mexico: United Bible Societies, 1987, p. 590.
277- United Bible Societies. God Speaks Today. The Bible with Deuterocanonicals. Old Testament. Proverbs. Popular Version. Second Edition. Mexico City, Mexico: United Bible Societies, 1987, p. 607.
278- The proverb recorded by Jorge Sintes Pros is: "Soon and well, never go together." In: Sintes Pros Jorge. Dictionary of Aphorisms, Proverbs, and Sayings. Barcelona, Spain: Editorial Sintes, 1954, p. 235.
279- Lao Tzu. Tao Teh Ching. In: Lin Yutang. Chinese Wisdom. Buenos Aires, Argentina: Colección ACADEMUS. Biblioteca Nueva, 1945, p. 39.
280- Feijóo Samuel. The Knowledge of Juan Without Anything. Signs in the Expression of the Peoples. Proverb. Santa Clara, Cuba: Signos Magazine, No 14. Year 5, No 2; January-April 1974, p. 110.
281- Valdés Jane Ernesto. Proverbial Divination of the Caracol and the Odun of Ifá. -In Cuban Santería- Documents for the History and Culture of Osha-Ifa in Cuba. Proverbs from (4-13) Iroso tonti Metanlá. First Edition: Proyecto Orunmila, 2007, p. 16.
282- Feijóo Samuel. The Knowledge of Juan Without Anything.

Signs in the Expression of the Peoples. Proverb. Santa Clara, Cuba: Signos Magazine, No 14. Year 5, No 2; January-April 1974, p. 173.

283- Feijóo Samuel. The Knowledge of Juan Without Anything. Signs in the Expression of the Peoples. Proverb. Santa Clara, Cuba: Signos Magazine, No 14. Year 5, No 2; January-April 1974, p. 156.

284- Solís José Antonio. Proverbs, Sayings, and Sentences. All the Treasure of Popular Wisdom from the Peoples of Spain at Your Reach. Spain: El Arca de Papel Editors, 2003, p. 57.

285- United Bible Societies. God Speaks Today. The Bible with Deuterocanonicals. Old Testament. Proverbs. Popular Version. Second Edition. Mexico City, Mexico: United Bible Societies, 1987, p. 598.

286- Cannobbio Agustín. Chilean Proverbs. Santiago de Chile: Encuadernación Barcelona, 1901, p. 73.

287- Lin Yutang. Chinese Wisdom. Buenos Aires, Argentina: Colección ACADEMUS. Biblioteca Nueva, 1945, p. 594.

288- Feijóo Samuel. The Knowledge of Juan Without Anything. Signs in the Expression of the Peoples. Proverb. Santa Clara, Cuba: Signos Magazine, No 14. Year 5, No 2; January-April 1974, p. 112.

289- Feijóo Samuel. The Knowledge of Juan Without Anything. Signs in the Expression of the Peoples. Proverb. Santa Clara, Cuba: Signos Magazine, No 14. Year 5, No 2; January-April 1974, p. 187.

290- Feijóo Samuel. The Knowledge of Juan Without Anything. Signs in the Expression of the Peoples. Proverb. Santa Clara, Cuba: Signos Magazine, No 14. Year 5, No 2; January-April 1974, p. 139.

291- United Bible Societies. God Speaks Today. The Bible with Deuterocanonicals. Old Testament. Proverbs. Popular Version. Second Edition. Mexico City, Mexico: United Bible Societies, 1987, p. 594.

292- Valdés Jane Ernesto. Proverbial Divination of the

Caracol and the Odun of Ifá. -In Cuban Santería- Documents for the History and Culture of Osha-Ifa in Cuba. Proverbs from (9-1) Osá tonti Okana. First Edition: Proyecto Orunmila, 2007, p. 35.
293- Valdés Jane Ernesto. Proverbial Divination of the Caracol and the Odun of Ifá. -In Cuban Santería- Documents for the History and Culture of Osha-Ifa in Cuba. Proverbs from (16-16) Merindilogún tonti Merindilogún. First Edition: Proyecto Orunmila, 2007, p. 67.
294- Valdés Jane Ernesto. Proverbial Divination of the Caracol and the Odun of Ifá. -In Cuban Santería- Documents for the History and Culture of Osha-Ifa in Cuba. Proverbs from (15-14) Marunlá tonti Merinlá. First Edition: Proyecto Orunmila, 2007, p. 62.
295- Valdés Jane Ernesto. Proverbial Divination of the Caracol and the Odun of Ifá. -In Cuban Santería- Documents for the History and Culture of Osha-Ifa in Cuba. Proverbs from (4-1) Iroso tonti Okana. First Edition: Proyecto Orunmila, 2007, p. 13.
296- United Bible Societies. God Speaks Today. The Bible with Deuterocanonicals. Books of Deuterocanonicals. Sirach. Popular Version. Second Edition. Mexico City, Mexico: United Bible Societies, 1987, p. 96.
297- The proverb recorded by Samuel Feijóo is: "Everyone plays their own hand." In: Feijóo Samuel. From Compliment to Saying, Oral Folklore of Cuba. Havana, Cuba: Editorial Letras Cubanas, 1981, p. 32.
298- Feijóo Samuel. The Knowledge of Juan Without Anything. Signs in the Expression of the Peoples. Proverb. Santa Clara, Cuba: Signos Magazine, No 14. Year 5, No 2; January-April 1974, p. 124.
299- Solís José Antonio. Proverbs, Sayings, and Sentences. All the Treasure of Popular Wisdom from the Peoples of Spain at Your Reach. Spain: El Arca de Papel Editors, 2003, p. 10.

300- Álvarez de los Ríos Tomás. The Book of Proverbs. Camagüey, Cuba: Editorial Ácana, 2017, p. 13.

301. Solís José Antonio. Sayings, Proverbs, Phrases, and Sentences. The Entire Treasure of Popular Wisdom of the Peoples of Spain at Your Fingertips. Spain: El Arca de Papel Editores; 2003. p. 10.

302. Solís José Antonio. Sayings, Proverbs, Phrases, and Sentences. The Entire Treasure of Popular Wisdom of the Peoples of Spain at Your Fingertips. Spain: El Arca de Papel Editores; 2003. p. 145.

303. Cannobbio Agustín. Chilean Sayings. Santiago de Chile: Encuadernación Barcelona; 1901. p. 21.

304. Flores-Huerta Samuel. Sayings or Proverbs. Thematic Compendium. Mexico: CopIt-arXives; 2016. p. 182.

305. Martí José. Notebooks of Notes. In: Complete Works, Vol. XXI. La Habana, Cuba: Editorial de Ciencias Sociales; 1991. p. 107.

306. Valdés Jane Ernesto. Prophetic Sayings of the Cowrie Shell and Odun of Ifá. In the Cuban Santería - Documents for the History and Culture of Osha-Ifa in Cuba. Sayings of (11-14) Ojuani Tonti Merinlá and Ojuani Tanshela. First Edition: Proyecto Orunmila; 2007. pp. 48, 90.

307. Valdés Jane Ernesto. Prophetic Sayings of the Cowrie Shell and Odun of Ifá. In the Cuban Santería - Documents for the History and Culture of Osha-Ifa in Cuba. Sayings of (4-7) Iroso Tonti Odí. First Edition: Proyecto Orunmila; 2007. p. 14.

308. Valdés Jane Ernesto. Prophetic Sayings of the Cowrie Shell and Odun of Ifá. In the Cuban Santería - Documents for the History and Culture of Osha-Ifa in Cuba. Sayings of (7-9) Odí Tonti Osá and Odí Sa. First Edition: Proyecto Orunmila; 2007. pp. 28, 85.

309. Valdés Jane Ernesto. Prophetic Sayings of the Cowrie Shell and Odun of Ifá. In the Cuban Santería - Documents for the History and Culture of Osha-Ifa in Cuba. Sayings of (7-9) Odí Tonti Osá. First Edition: Proyecto Orunmila; 2007. p. 28.

310. Valdés Jane Ernesto. Prophetic Sayings of the Cowrie Shell and Odun of Ifá. In the Cuban Santería - Documents for the History and Culture of Osha-Ifa in Cuba. Sayings of (8-1) Eyeúnle Tonti Okana and Ogbe Kana. First Edition: Proyecto Orunmila; 2007. pp. 29, 72.

311. The phrase by Tagore is: "I slept and dreamed that life was joy, I awoke and saw that life was service, I served and saw that service was joy." Tagore Rabindranath. Wikiquote. A Free Collection of Quotes and Famous Phrases. https://es.wikiquote.org/wiki/Rabindranath_Tagore

312. Martí José. Our America III. School of Arts and Crafts. In: Complete Works, Vol. VIII. La Habana, Cuba: Editorial de Ciencias Sociales; 1991. p. 285.

313. Sociedades Bíblicas Unidas. God Speaks Today. The Bible with Deuterocanonical Books. New Testament. Matthew and Luke. Popular Version. Second Edition. Mexico City: Sociedades Bíblicas Unidas; 1987. pp. 7, 71.

314. Vishnu Sarma. Panchatantra. Third Edition. La Habana, Cuba: Editorial Arte y Literatura; 2014. p. 198.

315. Valdés Jane Ernesto. Prophetic Sayings of the Cowrie Shell and the Odun of Ifá. In the Cuban Santería - Documents for the History and Culture of Osha-Ifa in Cuba. Sayings of (3-7) Ogundá Tonti Odí and Ogunda Dio. First Edition: Proyecto Orunmila; 2007. pp. 10, 101.

316. Martí José. Complete Works. Vol. II. Commemorative Edition for the Fiftieth Anniversary of His Death. La Habana, Cuba: Editorial Lex; 1946. p. 1843.

317. Confucius in: Lin Yutang. The Wisdom of Confucius. Buenos Aires, Argentina: Ediciones Siglo Veinte; 1952. p. 138.

318. Solís José Antonio. Sayings, Proverbs, Phrases, and Sentences. The Entire Treasure of Popular Wisdom of the Peoples of Spain at Your Fingertips. Spain: El Arca de Papel Editores; 2003. p. 150.

319. Martí José. Letter to José Dolores Poyo, New York, July 7, 1894. In: Complete Works, Vol. III. La Habana, Cuba: Editorial de Ciencias Sociales; 1991. p. 225.

320. Feijóo Samuel. The Knowledge of Juan Sin Nada. Signs in the Expression of the Peoples. Saying. Santa Clara, Cuba: Revista Signos, No. 14, Vol. 5, No. 2; January-April 1974. p. 186.

321. Vishnu Sarma. Panchatantra. Third Edition. La Habana, Cuba: Editorial Arte y Literatura; 2014. p. 268.

322. Lao Tse. Tao Teh Ching. In: Lin Yutang. Chinese Wisdom. Buenos Aires, Argentina: Colección Academus, Biblioteca Nueva; 1945. p. 29.

323. Cannobbio Agustín. Chilean Sayings. Santiago de Chile: Encuadernación Barcelona; 1901. p. 98.

324. Lao Tse. Tao Teh Ching. In: Lin Yutang. Chinese Wisdom. Buenos Aires, Argentina: Colección Academus, Biblioteca Nueva; 1945. p. 59.

325. Lao Tse. Tao Teh Ching. In: Lin Yutang. Chinese Wisdom. Buenos Aires, Argentina: Colección Academus, Biblioteca Nueva; 1945. p. 58.

326. Lao Tse. Tao Teh Ching. In: Lin Yutang. Chinese Wisdom. Buenos Aires, Argentina: Colección Academus, Biblioteca Nueva; 1945. p. 58.

327. Valdés Jane Ernesto. Prophetic Sayings of the Cowrie Shell and the Odun of Ifá. In the Cuban Santería - Documents for the History and Culture of Osha-Ifa in Cuba. Sayings of (2-1) Eyioko Tonti Okana. First Edition: Proyecto Orunmila; 2007. p. 5.

328. Lin Yutang. Chinese Wisdom. Buenos Aires, Argentina: Colección ACADEMUS, Biblioteca Nueva; 1945. p. 671.

329. Solís José Antonio. Sayings, Proverbs, Phrases, and Sentences. The Entire Treasure of Popular Wisdom. Spain: El Arca de Papel Editores; 2003. p. 74.

330. Feijóo Samuel. The Knowledge of Juan Sin Nada. Signs in the Expression of the Peoples. Saying. Santa Clara, Cuba: Revista Signos, No. 14, Vol. 5, No. 2; January-April 1974. p. 58.

331. Valdés Jane Ernesto. Prophetic Sayings of the Cowrie Shell and the Odun of Ifá. In the Cuban Santería - Documents for the History and Culture of Osha-Ifa in Cuba. Sayings of (14-3) Merinlá Tonti Ogundá. First Edition: Proyecto Orunmila; 2007. p. 57.

332. Valdés Jane Ernesto. Prophetic Sayings of the Cowrie Shell and the Odun of Ifá. In the Cuban Santería - Documents for the History and Culture of Osha-Ifa in Cuba. Sayings of (12-13) Eyilá Tonti Metanlá. First Edition: Proyecto Orunmila; 2007. p. 53.

333. Feijóo Samuel. The Knowledge of Juan Sin Nada. Signs in the Expression of the Peoples. Saying. Santa Clara, Cuba: Revista Signos, No. 14, Vol. 5, No. 2; January-April 1974. p. 142.

334. Feijóo Samuel. The Knowledge of Juan Sin Nada. Signs in the Expression of the Peoples. Saying. Santa Clara, Cuba: Revista Signos, No. 14, Vol. 5, No. 2; January-April 1974. p. 63.

335. The saying collected by Tomás Álvarez de los Ríos is: "As bad as not arriving is going too far." In: Álvarez de los Ríos Tomás. The Book of Sayings. Camagüey, Cuba: Editorial Ácana; 2017. p. 108.

336. Cannobbio Agustín. Chilean Sayings. Santiago de Chile: Encuadernación Barcelona; 1901. p. 20.

337. Solís José Antonio. Sayings, Proverbs, Phrases, and Sentences. The Entire Treasure of Popular Wisdom of the Peoples of Spain at Your Fingertips. Spain: El Arca de Papel Editores; 2003. p. 97.

338. Sociedades Bíblicas Unidas. God Speaks Today. The Bible with Deuterocanonical Books. Books of Ecclesiastes. Popular Version. Second Edition. Mexico City: Sociedades Bíblicas Unidas; 1987. p. 112.

339. Feijóo Samuel. The Knowledge of Juan Sin Nada. Signs in the Expression of the Peoples. Saying. Santa Clara, Cuba: Revista Signos, No. 14, Vol. 5, No. 2; January-April 1974. p. 130.

340. Solís José Antonio. Sayings, Proverbs, Phrases, and Sentences. The Entire Treasure of Popular Wisdom of the Peoples of Spain at Your Fingertips. Spain: El Arca de Papel Editores; 2003. p. 120.

341. Solís José Antonio. Sayings, Proverbs, Phrases, and Sentences. The Entire Treasure of Popular Wisdom of the Peoples of Spain at Your Fingertips. Spain: El Arca de Papel Editores; 2003. p. 120.

342. Martí J. Complete Works. Vol. II. Commemorative Edition for the Fiftieth Anniversary of His Death. La Habana, Cuba: Editorial Lex; 1946. p. 1669.

343. Solís José Antonio. Sayings, Proverbs, Phrases, and Sentences. The Entire Treasure of Popular Wisdom of the Peoples of Spain at Your Fingertips. Spain: El Arca de Papel Editores; 2003. p. 43.

344. Solís José Antonio. Sayings, Proverbs, Phrases, and Sentences. The Entire Treasure of Popular Wisdom of the Peoples of Spain at Your Fingertips. Spain: El Arca de Papel Editores; 2003. p. 13.

345. Feijóo Samuel. The Knowledge of Juan Sin Nada. Signs in the Expression of the Peoples. Saying. Santa Clara, Cuba:

Revista Signos, No. 14, Vol. 5, No. 2; January-April 1974. p. 152.

346. Valdés Jane Ernesto. Prophetic Sayings of the Cowrie Shell and the Odun of Ifá. In the Cuban Santería - Documents for the History and Culture of Osha-Ifa in Cuba. Sayings of (14-14) Merinlá Tonti Merinlá. First Edition: Proyecto Orunmila; 2007. p. 59.

347. Solís José Antonio. Sayings, Proverbs, Phrases, and Sentences. The Entire Treasure of Popular Wisdom of the Peoples of Spain at Your Fingertips. Spain: El Arca de Papel Editores; 2003. p. 20.

348. The saying collected by José Antonio Solís is: "Listen to the advice of everyone and follow your own." See: Solís José Antonio. Sayings, Proverbs, Phrases, and Sentences. The Entire Treasure of Popular Wisdom of the Peoples of Spain at Your Fingertips. Spain: El Arca de Papel Editores; 2003. p. 122.

349. Valdés Jane Ernesto. Prophetic Sayings of the Cowrie Shell and the Odun of Ifá. In the Cuban Santería - Documents for the History and Culture of Osha-Ifa in Cuba. Sayings of (6-6) Obara Tonti Obara and Obara Kana. First Edition: Proyecto Orunmila; 2007. pp. 22, 94.

350. Valdés Jane Ernesto. Prophetic Sayings of the Cowrie Shell and the Odun of Ifá. In the Cuban Santería - Documents for the History and Culture of Osha-Ifa in Cuba. Sayings of (11-10) Oluani Tonti Ofún. First Edition: Proyecto Orunmila; 2007. p. 47.

351. Valdés Jane Ernesto. Prophetic Sayings of the Cowrie Shell and the Odun of Ifá. In the Cuban Santería - Documents for the History and Culture of Osha-Ifa in Cuba. Sayings of (3-6) Ogundá Tonti Obara. First Edition: Proyecto Orunmila; 2007. p. 10.

352. Cannobbio Agustín. Chilean Sayings. Santiago de Chile: Encuadernación Barcelona; 1901. p. 36.

353. Valdés Jane Ernesto. Prophetic Sayings of the Cowrie Shell and the Odun of Ifá. In the Cuban Santería - Documents for the History and Culture of Osha-Ifa in Cuba. Sayings of (1-11) Okana Tonti Ojuani. First Edition: Proyecto Orunmila; 2007. p. 4.

354. Lao Tse. Tao Teh Ching. In: Lin Yutang. Chinese Wisdom. Buenos Aires, Argentina: Colección ACADEMUS, Biblioteca Nueva; 1945. p. 29.

355. Valdés Jane Ernesto. Prophetic Sayings of the Cowrie Shell and the Odun of Ifá. In the Cuban Santería - Documents for the History and Culture of Osha-Ifa in Cuba. Sayings of (5-15) Oshé Tonti Marunlá and Oshe Ka. First Edition: Proyecto Orunmila; 2007. pp. 20, 122.

356. Sociedades Bíblicas Unidas. God Speaks Today. The Bible with Deuterocanonical Books. Old Testament. Proverbs. Popular Version. Second Edition. Mexico City: Sociedades Bíblicas Unidas; 1987. p. 598.

357. The saying collected by Samuel Feijóo is: "The boa does not catch the hen while running." In: Feijóo Samuel. From Compliment to Witty Remark, Oral Folklore of Cuba. Havana, Cuba: Letras Cubanas; 1981. p. 33.

358. Feijóo Samuel. The Knowledge of Juan Sin Nada. Signs in the Expression of the Peoples. Saying. Santa Clara, Cuba: Revista Signos, No. 14, Vol. 5, No. 2; January-April 1974. p. 191.

359. Feijóo Samuel. The Knowledge of Juan Sin Nada. Signs in the Expression of the Peoples. Saying. Santa Clara, Cuba: Revista Signos, No. 14, Vol. 5, No. 2; January-April 1974. p. 152.

360. Sintes Pros Jorge. Dictionary of Aphorisms, Proverbs, and Sayings. Barcelona, Spain: Editorial Sintes; 1954. p. 127.

361. Feijóo S. The Knowledge of Juan Sin Nada. Signs in the Expression of the Peoples. Saying. Santa Clara, Cuba: Revista Signos, No. 14, Vol. 5, No. 2; January-April 1974. p. 29.

362. Álvarez de los Ríos Tomás. The Book of Sayings. Camagüey, Cuba: Editorial Ácana; 2017. p. 31.

363. Solís José Antonio. Sayings, Proverbs, Phrases, and Sentences. The Entire Treasure of Popular Wisdom of the Peoples of Spain at Your Fingertips. Spain: El Arca de Papel Editores; 2003. p. 16.

364. Feijóo Samuel. The Knowledge of Juan Sin Nada. Signs in the Expression of the Peoples. Saying. Santa Clara, Cuba: Revista Signos, No. 14, Vol. 5, No. 2; January-April 1974. p. 147.

365. Solís José Antonio. Sayings, Proverbs, Phrases, and Sentences. The Entire Treasure of Popular Wisdom of the Peoples of Spain at Your Fingertips. Spain: El Arca de Papel Editores; 2003. p. 120.

366. Feijóo Samuel. The Knowledge of Juan Sin Nada. Signs in the Expression of the Peoples. Saying. Santa Clara, Cuba: Revista Signos, No. 14, Vol. 5, No. 2; January-April 1974. p. 158.

367. Solís José Antonio. Sayings, Proverbs, Phrases, and Sentences. The Entire Treasure of Popular Wisdom of the Peoples of Spain at Your Fingertips. Spain: El Arca de Papel Editores; 2003. p. 129.

368. Feijóo Samuel. The Knowledge of Juan Sin Nada. Signs in the Expression of the Peoples. Saying. Santa Clara, Cuba: Revista Signos, No. 14, Vol. 5, No. 2; January-April 1974. p. 161.

369. Feijóo Samuel. The Knowledge of Juan Sin Nada. Signs in the Expression of the Peoples. Saying. Santa Clara, Cuba: Revista Signos, No. 14, Vol. 5, No. 2; January-April 1974. p. 54.

370. Flores-Huerta Samuel. Sayings or Proverbs. Thematic Compendium. Mexico: CopIt-arXives; 2016. p. 29.

371. Flores-Huerta Samuel. Sayings or Proverbs. Thematic Compendium. Mexico: CopIt-arXives; 2016. p. 30.

372. Sintes Pros Jorge. Dictionary of Aphorisms, Proverbs, and Sayings. Barcelona, Spain: Editorial Sintes; 1954. p. 306.

373. Sintes Pros Jorge. Dictionary of Aphorisms, Proverbs, and Sayings. Barcelona, Spain: Editorial Sintes; 1954. pp. 137, 210.

374. Sintes Pros Jorge. Dictionary of Aphorisms, Proverbs, and Sayings. Barcelona, Spain: Editorial Sintes; 1954. p. 285.

375. Solís José Antonio. Sayings, Proverbs, Phrases, and Sentences. The Entire Treasure of Popular Wisdom of the Peoples of Spain at Your Fingertips. Spain: El Arca de Papel Editores; 2003. p. 17.

376. Solís José Antonio. Sayings, Proverbs, Phrases, and Sentences. The Entire Treasure of Popular Wisdom of the Peoples of Spain at Your Fingertips. Spain: El Arca de Papel Editores; 2003. p. 141.

377. Feijóo Samuel. The Knowledge of Juan Sin Nada. Signs in the Expression of the Peoples. Saying. Santa Clara, Cuba: Revista Signos, No. 14, Vol. 5, No. 2; January-April 1974. p. 137.

378. Valdés Jane Ernesto. Prophetic Sayings of the Cowrie Shell and the Odun of Ifá. In the Cuban Santería - Documents for the History and Culture of Osha-Ifa in Cuba. Sayings of (12-2) Eyilá Tonti Eyioko and Otrupon Guede. First Edition: Proyecto Orunmila; 2007. pp. 49, 112.

379. Feijóo Samuel. From Compliment to Witty Remark, Oral Folklore of Cuba. Havana, Cuba: Letras Cubanas; 1981. p. 32.

380. Valdés Jane Ernesto. Prophetic Sayings of the Cowrie Shell and the Odun of Ifá. In the Cuban Santería - Documents for the History and Culture of Osha-Ifa in Cuba. Sayings of

(16-12) Merindilogún Tonti Eyilá. First Edition: Proyecto Orunmila; 2007. p. 66.

381. Feijóo Samuel. The Knowledge of Juan Sin Nada. Signs in the Expression of the Peoples. Saying. Santa Clara, Cuba: Revista Signos, No. 14, Vol. 5, No. 2; January-April 1974. p. 137.

382. Feijóo Samuel. The Knowledge of Juan Sin Nada. Signs in the Expression of the Peoples. Saying. Santa Clara, Cuba: Revista Signos, No. 14, Vol. 5, No. 2; January-April 1974. p. 205.

383. Solís José Antonio. Sayings, Proverbs, Phrases, and Sentences. The Entire Treasure of Popular Wisdom of the Peoples of Spain at Your Fingertips. Spain: El Arca de Papel Editores; 2003. p. 65.

384. Feijóo Samuel. The Knowledge of Juan Sin Nada. Signs in the Expression of the Peoples. Saying. Santa Clara, Cuba: Revista Signos, No. 14, Vol. 5, No. 2; January-April 1974. p. 200.

385. Feijóo Samuel. The Knowledge of Juan Sin Nada. Signs in the Expression of the Peoples. Saying. Santa Clara, Cuba: Revista Signos, No. 14, Vol. 5, No. 2; January-April 1974. p. 184.

386. Valdés Jane Ernesto. Prophetic Sayings of the Cowrie Shell and the Odun of Ifá. In the Cuban Santería - Documents for the History and Culture of Osha-Ifa in Cuba. Sayings of (10-14) Ofún Tonti Merinlá. First Edition: Proyecto Orunmila; 2007. p. 44.

387. Franklyn B. In: Clavel, Vicente. When Great Inventors Were Children. Havana, Cuba: Editorial Gente Nueva; 1978. p. 12.

388. Martí José. In the United States of North America. Letters, Painting, and Various Articles. In: Complete Works, Vol. XIII. Havana, Cuba: Editorial de Ciencias Sociales; 1991. p. 278.

389. Sociedades Bíblicas Unidas. God Speaks Today. The Bible with Deuterocanonical Books. Ecclesiasticus. Popular Version. Second Edition. Mexico City: Sociedades Bíblicas Unidas; 1987. p. 94.

390. Sociedades Bíblicas Unidas. God Speaks Today. The Bible with Deuterocanonical Books. New Testament. James. Popular Version. Second Edition. Mexico City: Sociedades Bíblicas Unidas; 1987. p. 253.

391. Confucius. In: Lin Yutang. The Wisdom of Confucius. Buenos Aires, Argentina: Ediciones Siglo Veinte; 1952. p. 187.

392. Epictetus. Maxims, Exhortations, and Advice. Barcelona, Spain: Biblioteca Orientalista, Editorial Teosófica; 1922. p. 131.

393. Valdés Jane Ernesto. Prophetic Sayings of the Cowrie Shell and the Odun of Ifá. In the Cuban Santería - Documents for the History and Culture of Osha-Ifa in Cuba. Sayings of (4-8) Iroso Tonti Eyeúnle, of (8-7) Eyeúnle Tonti Odí, of Ika Ogundá, and of Oshe Meyi. First Edition: Proyecto Orunmila; 2007. pp. 15, 32, 109, 120.

394. Vishnu Sarma. Panchatantra. Editorial Arte y Literatura. Third Edition. Havana, Cuba: 2014. p. 105.

395. Confucius. In: Lin Yutang. Chinese Wisdom, Buenos Aires, Argentina: Colección ACADEMUS, Biblioteca Nueva; 1945. p. 291.

396. Feijóo Samuel. The Knowledge of Juan Sin Nada. Signs in the Expression of the Peoples. Saying. Santa Clara, Cuba: Revista Signos, No. 14, Vol. 5, No. 2; January-April 1974. p. 159.

397. Valdés Jane Ernesto. Prophetic Sayings of the Cowrie Shell and the Odun of Ifá. In the Cuban Santería - Documents for the History and Culture of Osha-Ifa in Cuba. Sayings of (1-1) Okana Tonti Okana and Okana Meyi. First Edition: Proyecto Orunmila; 2007. pp. 1, 95.

398. Feijóo Samuel. The Knowledge of Juan Sin Nada. Signs in the Expression of the Peoples. Saying. Santa Clara, Cuba: Revista Signos, No. 14, Vol. 5, No. 2; January-April 1974. p. 87.

399. Valdés Jane Ernesto. Prophetic Sayings of the Cowrie Shell and the Odun of Ifá. In the Cuban Santería - Documents for the History and Culture of Osha-Ifa in Cuba. Sayings of (13-7) Metanlá Tonti Odí. First Edition: Proyecto Orunmila; 2007. p. 55.

400. Feijóo Samuel. The Knowledge of Juan Sin Nada. Signs in the Expression of the Peoples. Saying. Santa Clara, Cuba: Revista Signos, No. 14, Vol. 5, No. 2; January-April 1974. p. 52.

401. Feijóo Samuel. The Knowledge of Juan Sin Nada. Signs in the Expression of the Peoples. Saying. Santa Clara, Cuba: Revista Signos, No. 14, Vol. 5, No. 2; January-April 1974. p. 178.

402. Valdés Jane Ernesto. Prophetic Sayings of the Cowrie Shell and the Odun of Ifá. In the Cuban Santería - Documents for the History and Culture of Osha-Ifa in Cuba. Sayings of (1-1) Okana Tonti Okana. First Edition: Proyecto Orunmila; 2007. p. 1.

403. Álvarez de los Ríos Tomás. The Book of Proverbs. Camagüey, Cuba: Editorial Ácana; 2017. p. 88.

404. Solís José Antonio. Sayings, Proverbs, Phrases, and Sentences. The Entire Treasure of Popular Wisdom of the Peoples of Spain at Your Fingertips. Spain: El Arca de Papel Editores; 2003. p. 89.

405. Solís José Antonio. Sayings, Proverbs, Phrases, and Sentences. The Entire Treasure of Popular Wisdom of the Peoples of Spain at Your Fingertips. Spain: El Arca de Papel Editores; 2003. p. 109.

406. Feijóo Samuel. The Knowledge of Juan Sin Nada. Signs in the Expression of the Peoples. Saying. Santa Clara, Cuba: Revista Signos, No. 14, Vol. 5, No. 2; January-April 1974. p. 137.

407. Valdés Jane Ernesto. Prophetic Sayings of the Cowrie Shell and the Odun of Ifá. In the Cuban Santería - Documents for the History and Culture of Osha-Ifa in Cuba. Sayings of (12-16) Eyilá Tonti Merindilogún. First Edition: Proyecto Orunmila; 2007. p. 53.

408. Feijóo Samuel. The Knowledge of Juan Sin Nada. Signs in the Expression of the Peoples. Saying. Santa Clara, Cuba: Revista Signos, No. 14, Vol. 5, No. 2; January-April 1974. p. 53.

409. The saying collected by Julio Cesar García is: "What's past is past, but be aware of what's left." In: Feijóo Samuel. The Knowledge of Juan Sin Nada. Signs in the Expression of the Peoples. Saying. Santa Clara, Cuba: Revista Signos, No. 14, Vol. 5, No. 2; January-April 1974. p. 114.

410. Martí José. Complete Works, Vol. II. Commemorative Edition for the 50th Anniversary of His Death. Havana, Cuba: Editorial Lex; 1946. p. 1848.

~~~

AUTHOR INFORMATION

Arturo José Sánchez Hernández, born in Havana in 1970, is a physician specializing in Comprehensive General Medicine and Psychiatry. He has an extensive professional and academic career, supported by several publications focused on ethics and the theory of values.

With outstanding expertise in sexuality and psychotherapy for couples and families, Dr. Sánchez Hernández has dedicated part of his career to exploring these areas of mental health. He also stands out as the author of self-help and personal growth books, where proverbs and images play a central role.

Currently, he resides in Maun, Botswana, where he works as a psychiatrist at Letsholathebe II Memorial Hospital. His commitment to mental health and individual well-being has made him a highly respected professional both in his home country and in his new community in Botswana.

Discover more of my works at:

https://books2read.com/asanchez

~~~

www.ingramcontent.com/pod-product-compliance
Lightning Source LLC
LaVergne TN
LVHW041030150826
845672LV00001B/260

* 9 7 9 8 2 3 0 4 7 6 4 2 9 *